Praise for *How to be a Brilliant Mentor*

'How timely is this "guide" given all the studies showing the positive and accelerating impact a mentor can have on one's career, especially in today's fast-changing, web-driven global economy. That successful mentoring, which this book outlines, can be a win-win for both mentors' and mentees' personal and professional growth cannot be understated. Hang on to this road-map for your career's journey!'

Irene Natividad, President, Global Summit of Women

'A pragmatic guide for the braves who want to become people developers, beyond pretending this is a given by design for all managers.'

Armelle Carminati-Rabasse, Chief Resources Officer, Unibail-Rodamco

'Powerful and wise people have mentored others since the dawn of human history. Indeed, mentoring has always been an important way to pass on leadership skills and responsibility – down the generations. This book is an excellent account of this close relationship between becoming and performing for mentors, how managers can become mentors and thus enhance their own leadership abilities.'

Francesco Savio, Corporate Diversity Manager, Total Group

brilliant

how to be a brilliant mentor

PEARSON

At Pearson, we believe in learning – all kinds of learning for all kinds of people. Whether it's at home, in the classroom or in the workplace, learning is the key to improving our life chances.

That's why we're working with leading authors to bring you the latest thinking and best practices, so you can get better at the things that are important to you. You can learn on the page or on the move, and with content that's always crafted to help you understand quickly and apply what you've learned.

If you want to upgrade your personal skills or accelerate your career, become a more effective leader or more powerful communicator, discover new opportunities or simply find more inspiration, we can help you make progress in your work and life.

Pearson is the world's leading learning company. Our portfolio includes the Financial Times and our education business, Pearson International.

Every day our work helps learning flourish, and wherever learning flourishes, so do people.

To learn more, please visit us at **www.pearson.com/uk**

brilliant

how to be a brilliant mentor

Gisèle Szczyglak

PEARSON

Harlow, England • London • New York • Boston • San Francisco • Toronto • Sydney • Auckland • Singapore • Hong Kong
Tokyo • Seoul • Taipei • New Delhi • Cape Town • São Paulo • Mexico City • Madrid • Amsterdam • Munich • Paris • Milan

PEARSON EDUCATION LIMITED
Edinburgh Gate
Harlow CM20 2JE
United Kingdom
Tel: +44 (0)1279 623623
Web: www.pearson.com/uk

First published 2016 (print and electronic)

© WLC Partners 2016 (print and electronic)

Pearson Education is not responsible for the content of third-party internet
sites.

ISBN: 978-1-292-08816-7 (print)
　　　 978-1-292-08900-3 (PDF)
　　　 978-1-292-08902-7 (ePub)

British Library Cataloguing-in-Publication Data
A catalogue record for the print edition is available from the British Library

Library of Congress Cataloging-in-Publication Data
A catalog record for the print edition is available from the Library of Congress

10 9 8 7 6 5 4 3 2 1
20 19 18 17 16

Series cover design by David Carroll & Co

Print edition typeset in 10/14pt Palatino LT Pro by SPi Global
Print edition printed in Great Britain by Henry Ling Ltd, at the Dorset Press,
Dorchester, Dorset

NOTE THAT ANY PAGE CROSS REFERENCES REFER TO THE PRINT
EDITION

Contents

About the author

Gisèle Szczyglak is an Executive Coach, facilitator and author. She has a PhD in political philosophy and is the founder of a Franco-British company, WLC Partners. Gisèle has developed expertise in implementing mentoring programmes within companies and institutions. In 2014, she wrote the first toolkit on mentoring, published by Pearson in France: *Guide pratique du mentoring. Développez l'intelligence collective* [A practical guide to mentoring. Develop collective intelligence]. She has created a unique methodology for leading collective mentoring sessions, working in both the private and the public sectors. She has set up an association dedicated to mentoring – the International Mentoring Centre.

Through her company, Gisèle helps business, institutions and governments to adopt a new approach and maximise collective intelligence in order to increase performance and find innovative solutions.

Gisèle has developed a positive approach to help individuals reach their potential and to maximise talent within an organisation. Her company offers and facilitates discussions on topics relevant to companies, institutions and governments. WLC Partners runs tailor-made programmes and workshops on leadership, intercultural management and communication.

Acknowledgements

I would like to thank Steve Temblett, my editor, for his support and for trusting me. I am also grateful to his team for their work on this project. I would like to thank companies, institutions and all the mentors and mentees I have been fortunate to meet and to work with, in developing a positive mentoring culture together.

I would like to thank my sister Dominique for her unfailing support, Jagdeep Bajwa for her collaboration, and I would like to thank Jo Christian Waller for her valuable collaboration on this book.

Introduction

Where does mentoring come from?

The term 'mentoring' originates from Greek mythology, when Ulysses, King of Ithaca, leaving for the siege of Troy, asked his friend Mentor to take care of his son, Telemachus, and to become his teacher, adviser, guardian and friend. Ever since, mentors have performed this multi-faceted role, as fully-rounded individuals – as educators, they pass on values and knowledge, and as trainers, they share their experience and analysis of particular situations, to help the mentees they support. Throughout history, mentors have been political advisers, strategists, exceptional educators, inspirational figures, with or without an official title. Philip II of Macedonia entrusted the education of his son, Alexander the Great, to the philosopher Aristotle. Seneca was Nero's tutor and adviser. The character of the mentor evokes a particular attitude of listening, a benevolent presence without authoritarian challenge, passing on specific knowledge and experience of life, and offering guidance on ways of behaving and acting.

Mentoring today

Modern mentoring, as we know it today, emerged in the form of programmes for tutoring, defined by an active learning methodology, with the aim of gaining, developing and passing on skills. During the 1970s, this practice became formalised, especially within American universities, schools, associations and companies – growing in importance, uptake and influence during the 1980s and 1990s. Since becoming established, mentoring has successfully contributed to improving the performance of individuals and organisations, with programmes now adopted by three-quarters of the largest organisations in the US. Professional networks, business schools and institutions, established and start-up businesses – all are engaged in this unique method for empowering individuals and organisations.

Why is there such a craze for mentoring programmes?

Mentoring today is seen as a programme for professional and personal support, encouraging the sustainable acquisition of quality skills, transfer of expertise and knowledge, sharing of experience and cooperation. Mentoring can provide career development, improve professional relationships and resolve organisational and managerial difficulties. It can provide solutions to challenges and issues such as inclusion, diversity management, intercultural communications, intergenerational cooperation and sharing of interdisciplinary knowledge. Mentoring can enable individuals to adapt better to the constraints and challenges of their organisation, allowing mentors and mentees to share their experiences and solutions, in order to respond to the issues they meet in the field. It can help managers, leaders and directors to boost their careers.

Who is mentoring for?

Mentoring is for businesses, organisations and institutions seeking innovative responses to economic demands and to the changing world of work: competitiveness, cooperation, networking, transverse working, development of human potential, increased employability, gaining commitment and fostering the loyalty of colleagues. In an environment where change is a constant, mentoring plays a major part in supporting the transition and encouraging workers in their continuing personal development.

By offering mentoring programmes, organisations also nurture their brand as employers, exploiting a method that encourages freedom to change, promotes confidence, enables knowledge and experience transfer and increases performance levels. This technique also helps to create working environments that promote well-being.

Mentoring is for leaders, directors, HR departments, for all decision-makers and strategic players in organisations with the will and intention to establish innovative, effective and sustainable support practices. Mentoring is for employees seeking unique methods based on transmission and cooperation to achieve their objectives and to respond effectively to the demands of their organisations. Mentoring is based on transmission and cooperation in order to increase performance. Mentoring can be a real career-booster and tool for personal development, a positive means of empowerment for individuals and organisations.

PART 1

The what and why of mentoring

CHAPTER 1

What is mentoring?

How this chapter will help you

Many organisations and companies today implement mentoring programmes in their organisations. This chapter will help you understand what mentoring is and why it is acclaimed as a tool.

Mentoring is a tool for managing change in organisations, and an instrument for boosting personal and professional development.

When used and structured well, mentoring can offer a complete professional support process, adding value both for those who use the programme, whether mentors or mentees, and for the organisations that opt to offer it to their employees. It offers a wide range of advantages for managing change and developing skills within an organisation.

As an innovative methodology for professional development, mentoring programmes can offer a practical and effective response to the challenges faced by organisations regarding their human capital: attracting, holding and retaining talented people, developing personal performance, encouraging the commitment of employees, increasing their motivation and offering meaning. It can also support personal and cultural integration, offering leaders, managers and employees a support facility based on sharing and transfer of experience and skills.

Mentoring is also a powerful tool for managing change – it can be successfully deployed when there are projected changes of culture and managerial practice, when there are issues with leadership or strategy, or when new entities are being integrated, to help with forming and retaining a pool of talented people.

Mentoring can address a number of objectives, including cooperation and diversity, capitalising on the knowledge of the most experienced people in an organisation. Hence the popularity of mentoring programmes with so many companies. Mentors involved in mentoring programmes learn how to transfer their skills and expertise to new staff and those with less experience or with less knowledge of the workplace environment. Mentoring values diversity of experience and different professional cultures by involving and bringing together people who do not necessarily work together and who do not have the same profile or background. The diversity of those attending mentoring programmes has a positive influence on leadership and management models and helps the organisation to perform better and improve its working practices. Mentoring enables organisations to facilitate inclusiveness in terms of gender, age, experience and career path.

Companies looking for new, simple solutions to create a positive work culture and improve individual performance see mentoring as an asset. Mentoring helps organisations working on their management and leadership models. Your boss or your line manager and you do not appreciate the way you have been managed. In the workplace it might be difficult to identify good management practices or the values shared by your team, your manager or by the whole company. Mentoring is a good way to facilitate the understanding and assimilation of your organisation's culture and to share questions about leadership and management practices. Mentoring programmes encourage new ways of transmitting the values and culture of the organisation, so companies tend to retain their talented people and the knowledge of their skilled employees.

By encouraging a mentoring culture, companies contribute to the well-being of employees, offering them a unique support structure: the mentoring relationship. Mentoring programmes provide a relaxing and a stress-free relationship as there is no managerial hierarchy between mentors and mentees. As a mentee or as a mentor, you will be able to learn and to progress in different ways without pressure. Time management and flexible working are topics that can be set as mentoring objectives. Because involvement and motivation are common issues, companies try to help their employees to resolve problems with the dual-career or flexible working hours issue. Nowadays both men and women face the same difficulties and follow similar career paths. Balancing personal life and professional life is still a challenge. This issue directly affects businesses with a long-term investment in their employees. Mentoring encourages reflection on the way the workplace is organised, in areas such as the culture of presenteeism, teleworking, part-time working and consultancy, so that the work/life balance is optimised for all employees. This is one of the most important ways for mentoring to help the organisation work on new organisational models and find attractive ways to retain talent and staff.

In many ways, mentoring is a powerful tool. It facilitates inter-generational dialogue within an organisation and creates new networks by breaking down the common hierarchical barriers that everyone is aware of but no one has really tried to over-come. It is a good way to encourage creativity and innovation and to encourage people to communicate and to share their knowledge and their experience. People sometimes feel they are useless, under-employed, with no possibility of advance-ment. They feel stuck in their jobs with no prospect of a posi-tive future or career opportunities. Mentoring is an attractive means to increase the loyalty of skilled people and to get them involved and motivated.

Being part of a mentoring programme values people by increasing visibility and recognition, for encouraging professional development within an innovative support programme. If you have not shown how great you are or you could be, take the opportunity to mentor someone or of being mentored!

Mentoring is a booster as well, as it boosts the organisation itself. Mentoring helps professional development and empowers employees and managers so they can achieve their professional objectives and face new challenges. Are you willing to take yourself to the next level within your company? Do you still not understand why you are not as successful as you should be? Join a mentoring programme to get a clearer view of your priorities: your Dos and Don'ts in your day-to-day working life. Mentoring will help you to increase your skills.

In a nutshell, implementing mentoring within your company will enhance the values of cooperation and mutual support, will develop individual and collective well-being, and will recognise and highlight talented employees to increase their commitment in their working environment.

Through the mentoring conversation, mentors and mentees will learn to develop many skills that will be useful in their daily working practices, for instance, active and high-quality listening skills, management and leadership. Because there is no hierarchy between mentors and mentees, mentoring conversations will create a collaborative process of interchange that will encompass a wide range of professional situations and issues. The solutions emerging from these mentoring conversations will be immediately applied in their various professional activities and everyday situations. In a context where collaboration and teamwork are becoming vital to leverage competitiveness, organisations must find ways and means to create the leaders and managers they need. Mentoring as a tool will be very helpful both for companies and employees to work together on vision, managerial courage, strategy, emotional intelligence, motivation, ability, communication, commitment, risk management and decision-making processes. All these topics are strategic for driving and leading organisations along the right path and need to be discussed with employees from different managerial areas. This is all the more vital when there is a need for change within the organisation.

From this point of view, mentoring strengthens and enhances the motivation of teams and workers through free discussions and exchanges at different levels, no matter where people are situated in the hierarchy. People are key to organisations, and mentoring knows how to make the most of them in a very gentle, yet efficient way. We call it 'collective intelligence' but it is just a new way of being aware of the importance of what people do when they work – what they bring to their job in terms of skills, motivation, energy and involvement. Mentoring will also supplement existing HR development programmes by offering a new support option for workers.

---

brilliant exercise

Make a list of your main challenges in your organisation today. At the end of the book, you will be able to check how mentoring can help you with these. Describe the context and the situation:

My main challenges are:

1 _____

2 _____

3 _____

4 _____ ▶

5 _____

6 _____

7 _____

8 _____

 recap

Mentoring is an easy-to-use tool for professional support and a valuable aid for managing change in an unknown and uncertain context which today is the most current situation in organisations. As an individual, mentoring will help you gain confidence, develop your skills and improve your performance. Mentoring will create a professional development space that is free from the stresses associated with the usual organisational structure and power games. By choosing to implement mentoring programmes and therefore a mentoring culture, organisations will open up a new space, without barriers, attractive, free, welcoming and collaborative. Everyone will be able to benefit from it: participants in mentoring programmes, teams and colleagues, and the organisation itself – in the way it manages human resources, talents and business.

CHAPTER 2

What is the difference between coaching, mentoring and sponsoring?

How this chapter will help you

Coaching, mentoring and sponsoring are different ways to develop professionally. This chapter will help you understand what these three types of support are, and how you can make the most of them.

Have you already been coached? Do you know the main differences among coaching, mentoring and sponsoring? It is not that difficult.

If you choose the coaching option, your coach does not need to be an expert in your professional field. Your coach will not share their personal experience or professional experience with you. Nor does your coach speak about lessons learned during their own career. Why not? Because coaches cannot share knowledge about an organisation with which they have no connection (except in the case of an 'in-house' coach). Your coach has a fixed-term contract, a 'mission' with a specific target for which they will be paid, determined by a third party: your organisation or by you yourself, if it is a direct consultation. That is why the mentoring relationship is essentially different and does not share the same timescale. Mentoring programmes are wider in scope and have a different agenda.

Your coach may be a mentor, but not all mentors are coaches, with a specific professional training that qualifies them for their role.

Do coaches and mentees have something in common?

The mentor does, however, share the attitude of a coach, in this case, in the ability to listen and take a non-judgemental approach to the mentee as well as knowing the art of questioning that the mentor in particular is taught during the dedicated training undertaken at the start of the programme. This will not turn the mentor into a professional coach, however.

Who is the mentor?

The mentor is the person to whom you talk about yourself, about your experience, your needs and your objectives, within the interpersonal mentoring relationship. The mentor will provide counselling and will share their whole professional experience in order to help you to achieve your objectives. Your mentoring conversations will be relaxing, non-judgemental and efficient, as there will not be any hierarchical relationship between the two of you. Everything you say will remain confidential.

Who is the sponsor?

The sponsor is the person who will speak about you in influential settings, formally or informally. The sponsor will recommend you openly and will help you to be more visible, enhancing your positive reputation in the field, within your organisation.

 **brilliant** tip

What is the difference between a mentor and a sponsor? Let us have a look at how it works (Figure 2.1).

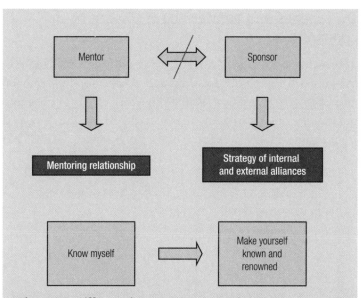

Figure 2.1 Difference between a mentor and a sponsor

The mentoring relationship will help you discover new solutions for everything you are facing within your organisation. You will learn how to analyse from a new perspective the professional issues and difficulties arising in your day-to-day routine.

Sponsoring will guide you to be more visible and to create your professional network in order to move forward. Developing a strategy of alliances goes with personal branding. Make the most of your mentor by enhancing your personal branding! Work on it with your mentor so that your mentor will be able to become your sponsor when required. Take a chance on it; get ready to meet new sponsors within and outside your company.

Have a look at Figure 2.2 overleaf. As you can see, mentoring and sponsoring are linked together, offering two effective routes to improve your skills and your performance. Be aware of how you use mentoring to find sponsors and increase your personal branding through your mentoring conversations.

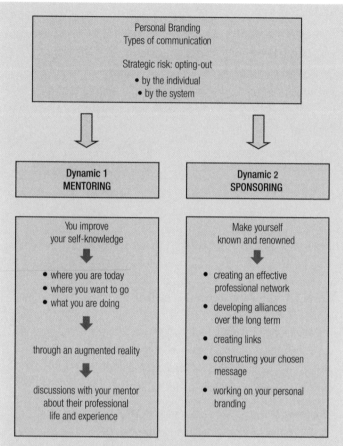

Figure 2.2 Mentoring and sponsoring dynamic

Have a look at what could happen if you do not consider the importance of personal branding

Personal branding is the primary means to achieve professional integration and recognition, through good self-knowledge and a strategy for promoting yourself and your actions.

If you do not take on board this philosophy of self-management and self-promotion, there are three possible options: (1) you will get tired and worn out trying and failing to gain recognition, lacking the essential dimension this dynamic imparts. In consequence, you will abandon the effort and exclude yourself; (2) the system will reject you, because of your failure to promote yourself; or (3) you will just stay afloat, simply treading water but without accessing any opportunities for personal development or achievement in your company.

In a nutshell, if you learn how to balance and how to manage these two dynamics – mentoring and sponsoring – you will succeed in the workplace. Mentoring and sponsoring will give you greater visibility, recognised and valued by your company. Without this visibility, you risk being ejected by the organisation itself, for example, you will not be promoted and you may experience the 'silent treatment' or even get yourself fired. Ultimately you may decide to leave the company after hitting a glass ceiling that stops you making any further progress.

Can my mentor be my sponsor?

Yes and no. It is not an obligation or a function intrinsic to the role and position of the mentor. Your mentor may be your sponsor, if this is what is decided within the context of the confidential relationship between mentor and mentee, and within the roles and positions defined in the mentoring processes. Indeed, mentors and mentees decide together on what 'comes out' of their exchanges. Mentors may be sponsors. Conversely, sponsors are not necessarily mentors.

Can I have a separate sponsor?

The sponsor relationship is based on forming links to nurture alliances, to serve specific professional objectives. Here are some examples of objectives where you might need sponsors:

winning a project, finding the right resources to roll out a project, implementing a strategy, managing change, making a move inside or outside the organisation, obtaining a promotion, obtaining access to strategic information and forming long-term links with facilitators and key individuals.

brilliant tip

The concept of sponsoring is vital to career progress, since over and above the essential skills gained through experience, co-opting, alliance-forming strategies and networking are all necessary levers for advancement.

There are three essential elements to achieve this objective:

1   Allow time: learn to know how-to-become

Your professional identity consists of the three traditional dimensions (knowledge, know-how and know how to be) but now a fourth, fundamental dimension is added: the dimension of time. This dimension involves the continuous assimilation and integration of information flows into your everyday professional life. Learning how-to-become implies learning how not to sink into passivity even involuntarily. Instead you have to keep yourself updated in order to keep your own job. You will need to learn how to manage your professional identity at all times and in all its aspects. Figure 2.3 shows the types of knowledge required in your professional identity map.

That is the reason why it is vital for you to build a qualitative network that will enable you to manage your knowing how-to-become in the best possible way. The first success factor is the qualification and management of a pool of potential sponsors and mentors. This is both a vital and a time-consuming process, whose benefits will be apparent in terms of benchmarking on other professional skills and on innovative practices in organisations and institutions. You need a more comprehensive benchmarking

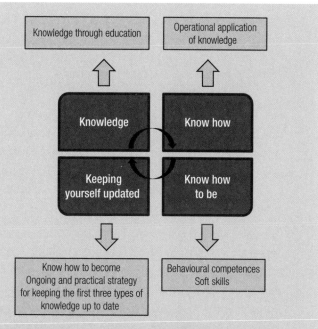

Figure 2.3 Construction of types of knowledge in the professional identity map

on social trends from contemporary movements, on what is happening in other companies that will help you understand upcoming events in terms of market and opportunities. You need formal and informal feedback on the quality of your own professional profile, a better understanding and perception of your new challenges, a broader, deeper understanding of the professional world. You also need to share contacts.

Identify now and evaluate how much time you spend supplying and maintaining this pool of potential sponsors and mentors inside and outside your company, and how you have 'blocked' it in your diary. Consider that your natural links and affinities will feed into an initial 'natural network', so in order to make your professional network fit for purpose according to your needs and objectives, you will have to establish it on other grounds than simple natural relationships from daily life, or on personal affinities.

2   Create a successful pool of sponsors and mentors

Why have a pool of sponsors and mentors? There is a contemporary need, linked to the present global context, for markets to be proactive, for you to maintain and upgrade your employability, to be your own 'driving force'. This takes place within a continuous process of managing your professional career path that obeys a kind of mutual imperative, arising both from market constraints and the consequences of burgeoning personal development.

You must apply self-management, constructing your personal career path as a dynamic entrepreneur both within and outside the organisation. Be responsible for your professional path, although as everybody knows, there is no real way to control your own destiny. We all are limited by a set of circumstances: coming first, or not, in a combination of situations. Be aware that there is an imperative to achieve well-being in our culture and society and to be always happy at any price. Being continuously happy and successful, showing how great you are in the workplace arises from a demand to comply with the rules of our culture and society. So hold back from this imperative, relax and take a deep breath. Because you cannot ignore it either, just do what you have to do to adapt to it in the best way you can.

3   A proactive desire for visibility

You have to accept that your professional identity will be 'externalised', your actions made public.

Show, comment and talk about the results of your actions, with a planned communication process regarding the missions and projects you have undertaken, your personal and team successes. This is an area in which it is not always easy to invest, since when you think objectively about what you do and your actions, you automatically assume some kind of visibility. This applies particularly to women, who often have the 'good student' complex, thinking that it is enough simply to do, in order to be 'seen', appreciated, valued, so that this translates immediately into added value in terms of professional development. It is an established fact, tested throughout your professional life: businesses and organisations are not neutral places where it is enough to be 'good' to reach the upper echelons[1] of the hierarchy.

A few useful things to remember for your career

Promoting your own actions creates influence. Promoting your own actions makes a contribution, highlights your share in the completion of successful projects. Broadcast, announce and spread good news. Create an ongoing, positive buzz around yourself to attract recommendations. Get yourself noticed, helping in the search for sponsors both as regards an effective message and in learning to communicate 'about nothing'.

Develop specific communications for your sponsors and your mentors

Consider three levels of communication. Your first level: communicating with high added value. Prepare your personal communications, your target group and recipients, your distribution points and your distribution media – on-line/off-line. Publicise within internal line management structures and in dedicated networks – internal and external. Then, distribute among current and potential sponsors – internal and external.

Consider your second action level: 'average' added value, which you use as a standard method belonging to a quality everyday process. Prepare your personal communications: incorporate a positive buzz around the action performed.

Highlight what seems 'normal' and 'commonplace' for you. Prepare your target group: your recipients and your distribution points. Publicise within internal line management structures and in dedicated internal networks. Distribute among internal current and potential sponsors.

Consider your third action level. There is no explicit added value here and you learn 'to communicate about nothing'. Prepare your daily personal message, including a positive buzz around the action performed. Highlight what seems 'normal' and 'commonplace' for you. Awaken a level of positive perception in the people around you about what you do every day: go to the 'meta-level': get an overview of the operational aspects of your professional life and observe yourself from afar. List what you do well in your daily life, and express it using simple sentences. You will lose the feeling of being pulled from one side or the other. You will no longer let a third person grab the victory that should be yours, even for elements, facts, professional situations, decisions that you consider minor, belonging 'normally' to your duties in the context of your job, and for which you are paid.

These three levels of communication are a kind of ethical way of managing competition, adapting to the demands of the environment and generating interest among your potential sponsors.

 'It is not the strongest species that survive, nor the most intelligent, but the ones most responsive to change.'

Think about these words of Charles Darwin when you create your buzz! It is not the strongest who succeed but those who are most adaptable. Be happy to be Darwinian!

The gift-exchange process in action

Understand the processes intrinsic to the way networks operate (professional, social, associations) and the golden rule based on one of the most basic rules of anthropological exchange in human societies: I can ask if I should bring something in return. My demand process is balanced by my contributor process. This is the power of the networks that form on-line and off-line communities. Once this logic is integrated, create transverse, vertical and horizontal lines of alliance in many circles within your networks, from the closest to the furthest, while bearing in mind that today's sponsors will not necessarily be there tomorrow, and those you do not have today look at line management levels above or slightly below N-1, N-2 or N-3 – may be there tomorrow.

Be smart and strategic: use the Pareto principle

The Pareto principle is the general method of sorting a problem issue or a subject into two parts, and making a distinction between the vital problems and the more secondary problems.

Applying the Pareto principle allows the properties of strategic problems to be identified and separated from the others. As regards time devoted to work, we observe that an efficient distribution of working time and its recognition consists of dividing the time according to the following rule: 80 per cent actual work and 20 per cent communication about carrying out the work. So adapt new rules: of 100 per cent of work supplied, devote 20 per cent to talking about it. This 20 per cent is not extra, it is part of the work itself. This 20 per cent allows you to create and develop the effective mentoring and sponsoring relationships you need to achieve your professional objectives.

▶brilliant exercise

Identify the people in your organisation who are important to you:

1 _____

2 _____

3 _____

4 _____

5 _____

What is your relationship with them?

☐ Sponsoring:

_____

_____

_____

_____

☐ Mentoring:

_____

_____

_____

_____

What lines of communication have you developed for:

☐ Finding mentors?

_____

_____

_____

_____

☐ Finding sponsors?

_____

_____

_____

_____

☐ Creating an effective professional network?

_____

_____

_____

_____

How much time do you spend publicising what you do?

☐ 5%

☐ 10%

☐ 15%

☐ 20%

☐ 30%

☐ more

Have you ever used the Pareto principle?

☐ Yes

☐ No

What should you do to apply it in your daily routine?

_____

_____

_____

_____

brilliant recap

In this chapter, you need to keep in mind the following points when making the distinction among coaching, sponsoring and mentoring.

1　You can develop with a coach, a mentor or a sponsor, depending on your objectives and needs, and the way you want to be trained.

2　You can be helped by a coach on specific points. Your coach, who is certified and an expert in providing professional support, has a fixed-term contract and is paid by your company or by

▶

you. Your coach will not share their personal experience or professional experience with you.

3 Your mentor is a professional like you. Your mentor comes from the same field as your company or from another company. Your mentor will share their personal experience or professional experience with you and will speak about lessons learned during their own career. Through your discussions, your mentor will guide you in clarifying and achieving the objectives you have set together at the beginning of the mentoring programme. Within this context, a mentoring relationship is different from a coaching relationship.

4 Your mentor will help you increase your personal branding, your visibility, and your success in alliance-forming strategies and networking. This is a key point in moving forward in your company. Your sponsor is someone who will speak about you in influential settings and will recommend you. He or she will build your professional reputation in a positive way.

5 Your mentor can be your sponsor, but not all sponsors are mentors. You need to look for mentors and sponsors inside and outside your company. This is the reason why you need to create a pool of sponsors and mentors and to work on your personal branding. Use mentoring to improve it! Don't forget to use the Pareto principle at the same time.

Note

¹ In organisational sociology, the Peter Principle expresses how selection and promotion of individuals work, with the levels at which competence limits are reached, ultimately harming organisations and individuals. According to this principle, each person tends to rise to their level of incompetence. This means that individuals may be 'ejected' from the system if they are either too incompetent or too competent: Laurence J. Peter and Raymond Hull, *The Peter Principle* (London: Harper Business, Reprint edition, 2011).

CHAPTER 3

How will mentoring benefit you and your team?

How this chapter will help you

It is essential to have a clear view of the aims of mentoring before going any further. This chapter will help you understand how you and your team can benefit from mentoring.

Mentoring relies on a precise methodology that frames the mentoring relationship throughout the programme, ensuring its ultimate success. This methodology enables mentors and mentees to understand better their respective attitudes, expectations, needs and objectives, in order to capitalise on the mentoring programme.

A personal, friendly relationship between equals, voluntary, and based on an ethic of trust

Mentoring is based on a voluntary relationship built on well-defined objectives, with an appropriate medium of communication. Mentoring is a win/win relationship, which is why it has become so popular in companies. This positive and easy methodology helps directors, managers and entrepreneurs, at different stages of their careers, to realise specific professional objectives and develop appropriate strategies. If you are not keen to become a mentor, sharing your global professional experience including your failures and your successes, do not even try! However, if you are willing to transmit, to share and to learn from someone else who will challenge you by asking you questions linked to their objectives, go for it! If you still have objectives that you cannot reach no matter what you are doing, just become a mentee!

Be aware that no one can be forced to be a mentor or mentee since the mentoring relationship relies on a mutual commitment: an authentic dialogue, developing trust as the programme proceeds and facilitating the sharing of key professional experiences – both positive and negative.

Mentoring is an interpersonal relationship based on an ethic of goodwill and confidentiality

Confidentiality is a vital condition of the mentoring relationship and a key factor in the success of the programme. Goodwill is also fundamental. Goodwill means, first and foremost, a favourable attitude towards the other person and a real interest in supporting them during the programme. As mentor, this implies a desire to share and communicate in an entirely non-judgemental way. As mentee, this means being willing to form the bond, starting from your main concerns and challenges. Mentoring is so effective precisely because of this deeply human aspect. Mentoring works because mentoring also addresses companies' own constraints while promoting personal performance, thus contributing to enhance the overall performance of organisations.

Mentoring will provide you and your team with professional support within a structured programme

Mentoring programmes last between 6 and 18 months. Most programmes are designed to last a year. The length of the programme means that the participants can invest fully in the process. As mentor, you will be able to measure and to observe the positive effects of the support you will be providing, and the results of your contribution. As a mentee, you will measure and evaluate the achievement of your own objectives. Objectives are a key element of the mentoring relationship. Established at the outset of the mentoring relationship, they constitute a contract between mentor and mentee, the keystone of their relationship and the common thread, in every sense, that runs throughout their exchanges.

Mentoring relationships will be based on equal, reciprocal and continuous commitment on the part of mentors and mentees within the relationship

Mentoring will mutually enrich mentors and mentees. As mentor you will contribute to the success of another professional, by sharing your own experience and lessons learned while also discovering other ways of thinking. As mentee, you will increase your chances of success, with the benefit of another person's experience and knowledge. You will also discover other ways of thinking. Mentors and mentees share responsibility for the success of their mentoring relationship that relies on their reciprocal commitment. They are jointly responsible for the success of the relationship, sharing their help, support and trust throughout the programme.

Mentoring will help you and your team to encourage solidarity and cooperation in the workplace

The mentoring relationship encourages mutual help and sharing of what mentors and mentees have in common and communicate to each other within their confidential exchanges. Learning to collaborate in this way encourages professional behaviour focused on cooperation. The organisation, the community as a whole, then benefits from this. Cooperation improves communication and well-being, increases efficiency and reduces stress. For instance, less time is lost in searching for information or the key person you need. Cooperation boosts the power of the network, a vital behavioural skill these days in the context of the global market with an ever-increasing number of contacts. The ability to create, use and nurture a network in the long term is essential in order to progress within an organisation.

 **brilliant** tip

Paradoxically, cooperation gives a competitive advantage.

The natural competition between individuals is better regulated with the establishment of cultures of collaboration that facilitate interchange, benefiting individual and global performance.

Mentoring is a very efficient way to spread the culture of your organisation and to build common values

By implementing mentoring programmes, you will have access to another way of looking at your organisation and the field in which it operates. The in-house mentoring programme brings together people who know their organisation well – often suggested as mentors – with people likely to be mentees who do not have the same knowledge or experience. By creating mentor–mentee pairings between people who would not normally interact at this level of relationship and communication in everyday life, the mentoring process contributes added value to the knowledge of the working environment. Mentoring is a very good way of integrating new members of staff, training 'younger' people, making them aware of the culture of an organisation new to them: its official and unofficial rules, its practices, its limits and areas of creativity. If you find a new job in another company or if you change your position within your current company, mentoring will help you better adapt to a new environment, in a professional and personal sense.

brilliant tip

Mentoring gives access to a radically different view of the organisation, the field of work, the performance and managerial challenges, that can overturn received ideas about job positions, skills and ways of working. This gives positive results in terms of innovation, collaboration, communication and performance.

Mentoring is a career development lever: make the most of it!

Mentoring is a real career booster, because it enables discussion about professional issues met in the field. It encourages progress and problem-solving through the enlightenment offered by the mentor. Mentoring opens doors within organisations, especially when mentors and mentees come from different working areas. In that way, mentoring develops a unique type of network, facilitates communication, sharing of experience and competence between people who would otherwise never meet within the more 'traditional' company networks.

Mentoring encourages openness: experiencing and learning about diversity. It is good both for you and your team!

Mentoring is a management tool breaking down barriers. It cultivates and nurtures diversity in a broad sense: the variety of professional profiles, multiple approaches and experiences, different points of view, various perceptions of the situations encountered that challenge both mentors and mentees. Mentoring reflects and demonstrates the richness of your people and what this resource can bring to your organisation as an internal lever to produce what we call 'collective intelligence'. Mentoring does not produce clones, but enables each employee and worker to rely on their own talents, whatever position they hold in the company. Mentoring contributes broadly to professional and human values. Mentoring will help you and your team to grow. Be aware of your added value and learn to use it. Make sure your team is aware of its potential and takes advantage of it.

Mentoring is a relationship promoting professional learning and personal development

Mentoring is a relationship leading to better understanding and analysis of the professional situations encountered. The mentoring relationship relies on a methodology that optimises dialogue throughout the programme and the frequency of meetings between mentors and mentees: clarifying needs, establishing objectives according to the professional context and the needs of the mentee, tracking progress for objectives established at the start of the programme, evaluating their feasibility. As a mentee, mentoring will help you to develop key behavioural competences. At the end of the day, mentoring enriches mentors and mentees involved in the programme at a personal level, increasing their understanding and ability to analyse any situations encountered.

Mentoring conversations are a specific form of dialogue, allowing feedback to be given and received outside of a line management relationship

The mentoring relationship is based on the quality and authenticity of feedback given by mentors away from any pressure or the managerial hierarchy. The consequent freedom promotes interaction and discussion on the feedback. This will help the mentee to receive it, and undertake their own plan of action.

Never forget the golden rules of management! Managers are supposed to evaluate actions performed by individuals, and not the individuals themselves. When mentoring methodology is applied in the right way, mentoring allows mentees to progress both in the professional arena and in their personal development, without feeling they are being evaluated.

brilliant tip

There is a different kind of management intrinsic to the mentoring process, expressed within a relationship external to the managerial hierarchy.

Mentoring story telling

Mentors and mentees will be sharing experiences and career paths and will be transferring their skills to each other.

As a mentor, you will share the variety, richness and authenticity of your experiences. You will explain the difficult situations you went through – failures, successes, and seminal moments. This sharing will mobilise you in a new way and will give you the opportunity to model your own path. You may use techniques such as 'story-telling' and the 'elevator pitch'.[1] You will pass on your best practices and will actively share them with your mentee. As mentee, you will be engaged in expressing your professional emotions:[2] expectations, desires, ambitions, problems and objectives. This free and authentic relationship, based on trust and confidentiality, increases the success of mentoring.

Mentoring is a great and effective tool for awareness-raising and support during changes in organisations

Because of its innovative methodology and its limited duration, mentoring can accompany and support strategic change in organisations. Whether it involves a redirection of managerial culture, structural changes after a merger, international development, integration of new communication facilities, new policies for inclusion and recruitment, changes at board level or managerial structure and strategy, mentoring as a tool helps companies to raise awareness of the challenges of the change. It facilitates understanding, assimilation and integration of the developments and transformations required.

 **brilliant** tip

Mentoring is an innovative tool for managing change.

Mentoring methodology is based on the action learning process that allows mentors and mentees to benefit from their mutual development

As mentors and mentees, you will both benefit from the mentoring relationship in terms of lessons learned. The knowledge gained comes directly from your shared questioning about your experiences and your career path within a symmetrical relationship. Mentoring is all about questioning experience itself and about what you can learn from it. The mentoring process is in some ways a very concrete experience.

brilliant tip

Mentors and mentees learn to learn from each other, by discussing their professional experiences. Mentors and mentees enter a control loop of knowledge and experience.

As mentors and mentees, you will learn to help and be helped. You will understand, formalise and discover your models, your beliefs and your limits in new ways, through shared development. You will deploy new resources for professional progress.

Theory questions experience in an action learning control loop (Figure 3.1). Experience questions the understanding gained and enriches the knowledge. As mentors and mentees, you will question the ways in which both of you have acquired knowledge and experience. You will find out your models together through mutual investigation of your real lives. You will discover together the way you have learned to learn and the way you have been trained during your professional career. Then, you will learn to learn together.

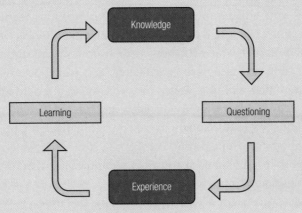

Figure 3.1 Action learning control loop

Whether you are a mentor or a mentee, mentoring will allow you to know yourself better, both professionally and personally, to model yourself, to receive feedback better, analyse and summarise your career path. Mentoring will be an opportunity to affirm yourself, to achieve your objectives in order to realise your ambitions. Through mentoring, you will be able to make progress in your professional skills, to express your talents and to flourish in a personal process involving listening and encouragement. You engage in a professional process of learning, analysis and capitalising on your talents, with support for change, within which you will learn so many key things to boost your career! You will expand your knowledge, define various career steps, validate and achieve specific professional objectives, find professional solutions and practices, work on your behaviour, develop appropriate strategies and consolidate professional growth. As a mentor, your main tasks will be to contribute to the success of another professional, to share your experience, expertise and the lessons you have learned and to discover other ways of thinking and acting. As a mentee, your major objectives will be to increase your chances of success, to benefit from another person's experience, expertise and knowledge and to discover other ways of thinking and acting.

By implementing a mentoring programme within your company, you will be innovative in supporting your teams and colleagues, offering a professional development tool acclaimed on the market. You will show your team and colleagues that you value and recognise their talents. You will choose a methodology that will be a vector for success and a tool to encourage agility. Mentoring is an easy and very efficient means for adjusting continuously to change, reorganisation, business challenges and integrating complexity. You will create a new network establishing mentoring communities that develop cooperation and improve performance.

If you take part in a mentoring programme, it will allow you to become a mentor and adopt the positive, challenging and rewarding attitude of a mentor. If you decide to be a mentee, you will get new insights into ways of establishing and realising your objectives within a specified time.

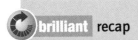 **recap**

In this chapter, these are the main points you need to bear in mind when you want to implement a mentoring programme.

1 Mentoring inaugurates a voluntary relationship between mentors and mentees. This relationship, which is at the heart of mentoring, is based on an ethic of trust, goodwill and confidentiality.

2 Mentors and mentees are equals. Mentoring requires reciprocal and continuous commitment from mentors and mentees within the relationship and the programme.

3 Mentors and mentees set their own objectives at the beginning of the programme. These objectives constitute a contract between the two of them.

4 Mentoring is a relationship promoting professional learning and personal development. Mentoring is a great tool for awareness-raising, for improving your skills and for boosting your career.

5 The mentoring methodology is based on the action learning process. Mentors and mentees learn to learn from each other, by discussing their professional experiences.

6 Mentoring will offer young professionals, employees, managers and teams professional support within a structured programme. Mentoring programmes last between 6 and 18 months.

7 Mentoring conversations are a specific form of dialogue, allowing feedback to be given and received outside of a line management relationship.

▶

8   Mentoring leads change in organisations.

9   The mentoring process provides mentors and mentees with a new kind of management, free of hierarchy. Your organisation will benefit significantly from the contribution of this new way of practising management.

Notes

[1] The elevator pitch is a means of communicating succinctly, offering a very brief account of one's professional work, career and talents in clear, striking language. It is the fastest way to create a contact and 'hook' the interlocutor. The context for this terminology is the following situation: imagine you are in a lift with the person you would most want to meet. Whoever you are: entrepreneur, manager, executive, employee, what would you say to this person in 40 seconds?

[2] See section 'Express your professional emotions', on p. 140.

CHAPTER 4

Individual
or group
mentoring –
what is best
for your team?

How this chapter will help you

This chapter will help you understand how to analyse what kind of mentoring programme is best for your company and team. When choosing a mentoring programme for your team, it is important to understand the objectives and challenges of individual and collective programmes. You need to clarify your company's strategy when an individual or collective mentoring programme is set up and present your objectives as manager: what do you want for your team? And you need to understand the individual strategy of future participants in these mentoring programmes. There are numerous benefits for organisations in the use of mentoring.

brilliant tip

The main advantage is the way that mentoring makes decision-makers aware of the multiple challenges faced by organisations. Mentoring programmes will allow them to understand and to be sensitive to what is really happening within their companies because people will share thoughts and feelings about their jobs and situations they would not share in another context. An innovative mentoring programme will enable them to truly express themselves and grow within the privileged space created by the mentoring relationship in order to develop and share their skills, benefiting from the experience and expertise of people of long standing in the organisation. Mentors and mentees will both widen their own networks, while helping to create another network within their organisation.

Why offer an individual mentoring programme?

As a mentee, you will discuss with your mentor the objectives that you will develop together, and build a plan of action. Through the mentoring programme you will increase the skills needed for professional practices applicable to your management, your leadership style and your communications. As a mentee, you will be able to set up new key strategies in order to achieve your objectives and deepen your understanding of the challenges of your professional environment.

Mentoring makes an active contribution to the construction of professional career paths and encourages personal development. Through cooperative construction of an augmented reality created by the mentoring relationship, mentors and mentees can stand back and watch themselves at work. The mentee's gaze allows the mentor to model a career path and experience. Having a mentor alongside for a specific period of time lets the mentee analyse situations thoroughly, determine objectives and build optimised action plans. The mentor turns a positive and authentic gaze on the mentee's career path. The mirroring of these two experiences is enriching for both mentor and mentee.

brilliant example

Here are some examples of what your mentoring objectives could be:

- Develop your career and set up an appropriate strategy in terms of internal mobility, to take yourself up to the next level, to broaden your scope while at the same time increasing your professional responsibilities, or preparing for your next promotion.

- Manage a professional transition.

- Find out how to recover, start again and continue in another direction after a difficult professional situation.

- Look for support and advice when taking up a position.

- Improve your managerial practices.

- Assert and sharpen your leadership skills.
- Perfect and adapt your communication methods and style.
- Enrich and develop your targeted professional competences.
- Deepen knowledge of your own profession.
- Explore other professions and sectors in your organisation.
- Integrate yourself into an organisation and assimilate its culture.
- Benefit from the experience and expertise of others.
- Receive feedback with no political agenda, or organisational or managerial hierarchy.
- Understand your own professional field: find the right keys to progress.
- Ask yourself the right questions.
- Develop your knowledge of how to be.
- Fulfil your potential.
- Comprehend, manage and optimise risk-taking.
- Increase your own visibility.

What are your needs as a mentee?

Here is a very focused exercise to help you to clarify your needs before attending and engaging in a mentoring programme. The following are key questions that you could also use to take stock of your current professional situation and to state adequate and useful professional objectives. Take the opportunity of mentoring to check where you are on your career path and to understand who you have become over the past few years; or who you still aim to be and what you are striving to do to reach your goals.

▶ brilliant exercise

Choose the items from this list that echo your current situation and match your needs. Write them down on a piece of paper and start working on them, asking yourself what is at stake for each item.

▶

Career development

- Where are you today?
- What is your path?
- What is the foundation for your career?
- What are you aiming at?
- Have you identified your position +1?
- Do you have projects in hand for the next two years? Are they clearly identified?
- Do you have a vision for the next five or even ten years?
- What is your satisfaction index, thinking about your career and your future? What score would you give yourself, on a scale of 1–10?
- What are your indicators for success?

Promotion

- When were you last promoted?
- What promotion are you planning, and what is the timescale?
- What kind of actions have you put in place to be promoted?
- Are you awaiting a promotion, and since when?
- Do you compare yourself with your colleagues?
- Do you have a strategy for being approached?
- What is your visibility index combined with your personal performance indicators?

Career transition

- Are you planning a new type of professional work?
- Are you changing your position, business and sector?
- Are you returning to work after a specific period of leave?
- Do you have a well-defined action plan, heading to a destination?

Support for change

- What would you like to change today in your current position?
- With which specific changes do you want support?

- What would you like to keep?
- What would you like to give up?
- What do you want to develop?
- What are your means? Your resources?
- What timescale do you give yourself?

Managing the double career

- Has the development in your partner's career affected the progress of your own?
- How do you assess this impact?
- What solutions and advice are you looking for?
- How would you like to develop today?
- How do you balance or prioritise managing your career with that of your partner?

Internal mobility

- Do you know what options are available for mobility within your organisation?
- Do you know how to identify opportunities?
- Do you have the right network and resources to achieve higher goals?

Time management

- How do you manage your time?
- Do you know how to prioritise, plan, delegate?
- What do you need to optimise your own time management?

Management

- Does your current position involve managerial responsibilities?
- What is your experience of management: matrix and transverse management and /or management in project mode?
- How would you describe your current practice?
- Which aspects of management and which situations would you like to discuss?

▶

Intercultural management

- What, in your view, is intercultural management?
- In what environment or professional context are you developing?
- What types of diversity are you familiar with?
- Which aspects of intercultural management and which situations would you like to discuss?

Leadership

- What, in your view, constitutes leadership?
- Do you know your own leadership style?
- How do your colleagues see your leadership?
- Are you recognised for your leadership?
- What situations and practices would you like to discuss?

Self-affirmation/self-marketing

- Do you affirm yourself enough within your professional setting?
- Do you have a message that allows you to affirm yourself?
- What images do you promote of yourself?
- What is your reputation?
- How do you perceive the image you project of yourself?

Networking

- Do you have one or more networks? Internal? External?
- How would you define the type of your network or networks?
- How much time do you spend creating an effective network?
- Do you consider that you get a good return on your investment?
- Do you have an on-line identity?

Communications

- How do you communicate in your daily life?
- Are you understandable and effective in the messages you want to give to your colleagues?

- What type of communication do you use in your networks?
- What are the contexts in which your communications have an impact?

Development of political sense and knowledge of the field: rules of the game within the professional context

- How do you analyse your working environment?
- What knowledge do you have of your 'field'?
- Are you able to decode your environment?
- Do you know the formal and informal rules that govern your organisation?
- Do you have the right set of behaviours?

Inter-personal relationships (line management, colleagues, clients, suppliers, partners)

- What relationships do you build and maintain with your line management, colleagues, clients, suppliers and partners?
- What qualifiers do you use to define these relationships?
- What would you like to change or improve in the current dynamic of your professional relationships?

Managing competition and competitiveness (internal/external)

- How do you handle natural competitiveness, peer competition and outside competition?
- What is your tolerance threshold for stress and pressure?

Exploring other positions and responsibilities within your organisation: a bird's-eye view of your organisation

- Are you familiar with the diversity of professions practised in your organisation?
- What would you like to learn about, understand and/or experience as professions, positions, jobs or sectors within your organisation?
- How do you broaden the knowledge you have of your professional environment?

- What are your needs in this area, and for what purpose?
- What do you know about your organisation?
- How do you locate yourself in the ecology of your working environment, to make progress and move forward?

Life–work balance

- How do you evaluate your life–work balance?
- How do these different lives interact?
- Is the partitioning satisfactory?
- Do you work part-time, or do you consider doing so?
- Do you know exactly what impact this arrangement would have on your career?

Risk-taking

- What constitutes risk-taking for you?
- What constitutes successful risk-taking?
- What experience do you have in this?
- What criteria would you use to define a positive risk-taking experience?
- What aspects would you like to discuss?

Organisation of work

- How do you organise yourself?
- What do you need to optimise management of your tasks?
- Are you satisfied with how you control your diary?
- What, in your view, is prioritising?

Managing stress and pressure

- What are your tolerance thresholds?
- How do you stand up to pressure?
- What are your working methods?
- What environment do you need in order to be productive?
- How do you let go?

- How do you find new resources and ways to move forward and keep going?
- What are your risk factors and your limits?
- How do you recharge your batteries?

All these questions will help you to define what your needs as a mentee could be and what kind of objectives you could set before engaging in a mentoring programme. Your answers will also be good indicators to show you what you have to work on to move forward and to reach your professional objectives. What do you really need today? Creating wider networks? Better management practices? Improving your communications? Increasing your impact? Developing your leadership? Sharing thoughts about your career path? Extending the knowledge of your organisation? Understanding the decision-making process? Learning to take the right risks at the right time? Getting promoted? Applying for a new position? Working for a foreign subsidiary? By answering the questions, you will start to understand where you are today. Write down and keep your answers. Read them through three times at least and ask yourself: What I am going to do now? How will I improve my situation and find the right solutions? To whom am I going to speak? When you have finished reading the book, either you can join a mentoring programme or you can make an appointment with your manager or your HR department.

Individual mentoring appears as a journey following defined stages (Figure 4.1). From stage 1 to stage 4, individual mentoring programmes are organised and designed by the company in collaboration with the external expert who helps to implement the programme and who has the required expertise. From stage 5 to stage 10 you have to follow the mentoring journey and to be prepared and trained for each stage, whether you are a mentor or a mentee.

It is always easier to comply with the mentoring key stages and mentoring ethics when methodology and processes have been sufficiently clarified at the beginning of the programme as an upstream phase. That is why before engaging in the individual

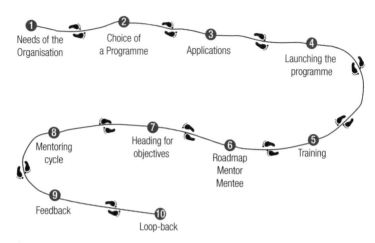

Figure 4.1 Mentoring road map

mentoring journey, you have to clarify why you want to attend this programme and what your objectives could be.

You could even try to explore collective mentoring and understand how it works as well. Collective mentoring will provide you with another kind of support and you will benefit from it in a different way.

Why offer a collective mentoring programme?

The second and very innovative form of mentoring is collective mentoring. Collective mentoring involves sessions bringing together groups of mentors and mentees. Before the meeting, the mentees suggest a specific topic whose issues will be addressed by several mentors during the collective mentoring session. This approach considerably enhances the wealth of solutions found and makes the sessions immediately useful and effective. Collective mentoring is a powerful tool for capitalising on the collective intelligence available – meaning all the participants – and so accelerating learning, transmission and sharing of knowledge and best practices.

What is the mentee's place in a collective mentoring session?

Consider the aspects involved in the collective mentoring process for the mentee. Collective mentoring combines and integrates the mentee's personal investigation axes into the group dynamic for construction of their professional identity and the objectives to be faced. Collective mentoring will mix and integrate these two combinations: the professional environment of the mentees and their personal ecology.

Have a look at Figures 4.2 and 4.3.

Integration of the first axis

The set of external parameters that affect the dynamic of the mentee's professional development and steer change.

Every organisation is a multi-dimensional integration system of several dynamic, changing and fluctuating complexities, aimed at producing performance. The unpredictability of this system, relying as it does on objective criteria, both structured and informal, makes it difficult to understand and decode, because of its potential impenetrability and the need for continually renewed understanding.

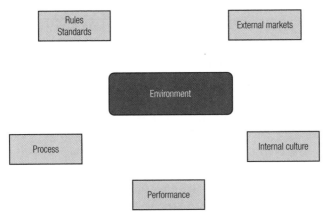

Figure 4.2 Mentee's professional environment

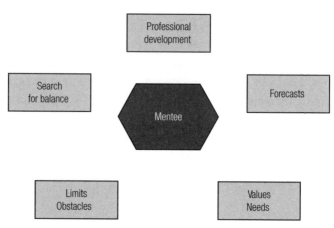

Figure 4.3 Mentee's ecology

Integration of the second axis

The mentee's professional dynamic is a set of parameters nurturing change. In turn, the mentee produces a complex system consisting of their professional identity, their place in the organisation, and the criteria based on needs, values and aspirations. This is the system within which the mentee constructs and develops their professional objectives.

Combination of the two axes

The mentee seeks to achieve internal professional coherence with the expectations of their environment (Figure 4.4). This internal coherence demonstrates the viability of the system and the setting in which the individual develops and settles, taking account of the present dimension: what they are, the multiple constraint factors of the environment and a forecast for the future.

How does this differ from individual mentoring?

Collective mentoring will offer personal collective support and will allow you to interact with several 'companions on the journey': several mentors and several mentees as well.

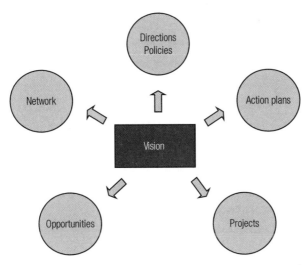

Figure 4.4 Interaction between professional environment and mentee's ecology

Collective mentoring will put you at the centre of a mixed community consisting of mentors and mentees and at the heart of a differential space-time that enhances your initial demand, completed by the questioning of other mentees and deepened by the contributions of mentors with their multiple voices.

As you can see, collective mentoring implies different dynamics and benefits.

brilliant impact

Collective mentoring exploits several levels: individual growth amplified by the growth and dynamic of a group, an effective analysis framework within a specific time period and a search for versatile and practical solutions with regard to the subjects handled. Collective mentoring relies on collaborative learning of the dynamic intrinsic to the nine characteristics of groups:

1 *Interactivity*: primacy of the relationship, extending the network dimension.

2 *Needs*: identification of a common denominator to develop objectives.

3 *Belonging*: members of a group are aware of their existence as a group.

4 *Interdependence*: members of a group are linked by alternating inclusive-exclusive relationships.

5 *Interaction*: members influence each other and respond to each other via the communication process.

6 *Cohesion*: members want to be part of the group, contributing to the direction, objectives and practices of the group.

7 *Social organisation*: a group is a social unit.

8 *Standards and rules*: a group develops rules and formal and informal standards.

9 *Archetype and symbol*: a group produces a number of representations – references that contribute to its coherence at the symbolic level and build a system of analogue correspondences between the lived experience of the participants in the group and the formal expression of its productions.

Mentors and collective mentoring

As mentors, you will have to comply with the specific features of collective mentoring, relying on your ability to listen to all members of the group – the other mentors and the mentees who bring the subjects considered – as well as on your ability to go further in decoding and analysing the topics covered.

brilliant tip

Consider that sharing knowledge and experience is always a gift of yourself – limited of course by the perception you might have of yourself, as it is impossible to perceive everything about yourself, or to be everything. This is still a positive limitation since it is illuminated by the experience and contribution of others. During collective mentoring sessions, the perception you will have of your own limits will then become a strong point, an anchor for others – both mentors and mentees – and a real source of learning. So do not limit yourself by not sharing your thoughts, opinions and experience!

As mentors, you will need to take time to reflect on the terms defining your prior commitment to the programme. Your main functions are as follows:

- to offer a process of interactions based on confidentiality, authenticity and goodwill;
- to share knowledge, expertise, perception and intuition;
- to be a role model, choosing key elements in your own career path, applicable to the subjects covered;
- to accept challenge from other mentors;
- to discover other ways of analysing and thinking about situations;
- to contribute to the plurality of solutions found;
- to listen to mentees with care and attention;
- to find out from mentees what they are asking for;
- to give support and encouragement;
- to contribute to the professional development of mentees;
- to support them through change;
- to learn to give help in a hierarchy-free environment.

Mentees and collective mentoring

As mentees, you will have to take time to reflect on the terms defining your prior commitment to the programme. As mentees, you will have to comply with the specific features of collective mentoring, relying on your ability to listen to all members of the group – the other mentors and the mentees who bring the subjects considered. You will also develop your ability to clarify your needs, probe your perceptions and deepen analysis of subjects covered to move on in your professional development.

Your main functions are as follows:

- to offer a place for discussions based on confidentiality, authenticity and goodwill;
- to identify your needs and clarify your demands;
- to welcome feedback from all the mentors;
- to welcome the insights of other mentees;
- to share your thoughts freely;
- to transform the content of the interactions into action plans;
- to commit to a positive dynamic of change;
- to learn to help and be helped;
- to discover other ways of analysing, thinking about and resolving situations.

What is the specific collective mentoring dynamic?

The collective mentoring group dynamic is based on the following elements: multiple knowledge acquisition developing a specific group leadership that involves cooperation, communication, team-orientation and inclusiveness. The collective modelling uses two lines of development: (1) a tendency to create values; and (2) a propensity to develop markers and signs of recognition. Collective mentoring will use the ability to shape useful archetypes and to share discussion as a way of testing and validating how an idea conforms to its representation in reality and how the group appropriates it. The group of participants will be influenced at the 'macro-level' – meaning the influence created by all the individuals considered as a whole group. Indeed, leadership is essentially an interactive practice, measuring its impact and effectiveness on what the others become under the effect of its influence.

- As participants, you will be using your own individual leadership in terms of authenticity, self-control, projection and initiative, developing individual modelling from the influence of the other individuals as well. We call it 'influence at micro-level'.

- The collective mentoring group develops a strong relational dynamic that recognises your own emotions and those of others as essential indicators to analyse facts and what is really happening in your work arena. Professional emotions are a personal compass within the group and a language to decode, not to reject. These decoded emotions also allow better acquisition of your social skills, better self-management of your mental maps and models that help you progress towards your objectives.

☀ brilliant tip

In terms of skills acquisition and development, you must value interpersonal links within the group in order to capitalise on the skills gained. If you can take part in the highly integrated relational dynamic of a collective mentoring group, it then becomes easy for you to learn and analyse, to express your emotions towards the professional and concrete situations described and to discuss the way you learn to learn.

The skills gained in these collective mentoring learning sessions are statistically more likely to be fully adopted by the individual. They increase capacity for adaptation to change and the integration of new data. They speed up the capacity to accept necessary changes: those you will have to lead yourself and that are the reason for your attendance at a collective mentoring session.

During the discussions in the collective mentoring session: you will confirm, reformulate or reorient modifications and adjustments to be applied and assimilated in terms of know-how, know-how-to-be and/or know-how-to-become. That is the reason why collective mentoring discussions facilitate cognitive learning of the many solutions suggested and strengthen analytical capacity for decoding complex situations.

Collective mentoring sessions facilitate an efficient attitude towards 'followership'. You will learn to show positive ability to 'follow', in a pro-active way. You will learn to develop the ability to integrate the group advantages and the ability to capitalise on the best. This followership attitude encourages specific skills based on the will to cooperate in order to achieve the objectives set by the group: authenticity, willingness to express personal ideas, ability to suggest, cooperation, cohesion, adhesion, a positive attitude, even in the event of conflict and efficiency.

What are the benefits of collective mentoring?

The benefits of collective mentoring arise from a high-quality group dynamic based on the profiles of the mentors and mentees, a clear and accurate identification of needs translated into topics, and the quality of the group leadership. The expertise of the external facilitator who leads and guides the mentoring group is very important as it requires strong competences in leading groups and in being able to synthesise all the thoughts and proposals that could emerge from the session.

These are the generic benefits of collective mentoring for mentors and mentees.

Developing leadership and visibility

Your personal growth towards leadership takes place at three levels (Figure 4.5). At an individual level, you will ask yourself: how can I perceive my contribution to the group, my impact as a vector of empowerment for others and myself? At a collective inter-individual level, you will try to understand how others perceive who you are and identify your level of contribution and influence – your degree of empowerment and your ability to create an environment that makes this type of dynamic possible. At a collective meta-individual level, you will ask yourself again: how does my leadership fluctuate through our group structure, independent of the individuals who compose it?

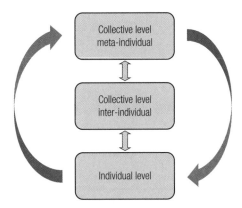

Figure 4.5 The three levels of personal development towards leadership in a collective mentoring session

Covering professional topics, subjects taken directly from the field and from experience

Whether you are a mentor or a mentee, you have to deal with major issues and situations met by organisations in the field. Collective mentoring sessions maximise affinity with the situation on the ground, increase effectiveness and maintain a practical attitude. Mentors and mentees come together to discuss subjects and questions that reflect their difficulties, investigations, projects and expectations, on which group reflection allows multiple solutions and developments to be worked out for current and future needs. Mentors and mentees together build a diagnostic of analysis and an objective process to discover the best collective and individual solutions.

Benefiting from overlapping solutions and viewpoints

Mentors and mentees together will share problems found, solutions implemented and successes with others taking part in the programme. They will benefit from practical and effective tools, that are immediately applicable. In that way, collective mentoring is a tool for solving situations by using the intelligence and resources of all the people engaged in the session. Collective mentoring is a very useful tool as it will allow you to benefit from practical and effective methods, immediately applicable in your daily routine.

Collective mentoring implements the interaction of two continuous processes:

- mentor dynamic: input and analysis line;
- mentee dynamic: questioning and hypothesis line.

Multiplying the viewpoints and the all-round handling – a 360-degree view – of subjects, together with the dual input logic of contributions and needs, ensures a richness and effectiveness that are unique to collective mentoring. Sharing is a vital prerequisite of successful collective mentoring. Mentors and mentees share what experience has taught them, the best and successful as well as the toughest, and new ideas and approaches deployed and produced during the collective mentoring session.

Collective mentoring increases communication and openness, and develops workplaces that are conducive to innovation and forward-looking dialogue,[1] whether about practices (management, leadership, communication), attitudes (behavioural and soft skills), investigation of career management (mobility, promotion, etc.), or problems relating to the development of organisations, business topics and the world of entrepreneurs – intrapreneurial[2] and entrepreneurial skills. Collective mentoring will help you to move forward through role-play and feedback.

Identifying talent

Collective mentoring is a catalyst for individual and collective talent. It speeds up identification of solutions suggested by group members and offers a context for discussion that leads to personal appropriation and assimilation of responses and results.

Transferring and developing skills within an action learning process

Collective mentoring, like individual mentoring, is a tool based on action learning. As mentors and mentees, you will learn to learn from the multiplicity and quality of the analyses about your professional experiences. The investigation and study of situations, subjects and issues are focused on decision-making and action plans. Collective mentoring methodology strengthens your professional identity, develops your performance, guides discussion towards resolution and encourages new learning processes. Collective mentoring boosts and speeds up your performance development, allowing multiple answers to be found for professional problems, and adapting them to suit your own needs and your working environment. It leads to the rapid assimilation of the changes to be undertaken.

Understanding the tools for developing empowerment

You will be able to develop both professionally and personally. Collective mentoring creates multi-voiced toolkits, a collection of practical resources ready for use according to the needs of the situation. It nurtures your professional and your personal development, encouraging self-knowledge, opening others up to understanding and enabling a better grasp of situations. It teaches positive empowerment for your own actions, the use of your potential and self-affirmation and expression as an individual within the group – in terms of contributions made, expression of your needs, clarification of your demands and dynamic of discussions.

By attending collective mentoring sessions, you will be moving forward through role-play and feedback. At the beginning of the sessions, you might play the role of mentee. Then, through the positive mentoring dynamic you will be able to gain mentoring skills yourself and become a mentor. Collective mentoring offers circles for discussion with ample contributions, areas for experimenting on all the theoretical and practical input, a laboratory of ideas combining praxis and theory, creativity and case studies, for both personal and collective development. This is the reason why, depending on the topic addressed, you might gain mentoring skills during the collective mentoring session.

What are the benefits of the collective mentoring for the organisation?

Collective mentoring will provide your company with efficient support to improve change management. Typically, collective mentoring sessions will help you to raise awareness of action plans to be implemented and how to develop your colleagues' motivation and commitment. When managing change, collective mentoring sessions will allow your teams to develop a better assimilation of values new to your organisation, and a clearer understanding of the general strategy. You can also use collective mentoring sessions to talk about the possible choices of different professional practices and new ways of working. If you choose to create new positions within your organisation, after merger and acquisition, for instance, you could also use collective mentoring to check if everyone has the correct perception of their particular role and position. Indeed, collective mentoring sessions are a very efficient means to work on the perception of your own position and skills and to question your place within the organisation.

From a business perspective, collective mentoring sessions could be used when it is time to develop a strategy to steer the organisation towards new markets – or if you aim to establish worksites for forecasting and innovation. You could put collective mentoring groups in a think-tank role when you are searching for new markets, or organisational models relating to new management and leadership practices, vision and aspirations, etc.

These 'collective' mentoring sessions, are above all ways of brainstorming and increasing performance within your organisation. You, your colleagues and teams will learn how to work better together. You will learn to be a group and a team, how to be an individual within a group and a team, how to handle your own position and integrate contributions from others, and how to create positive, effective group dynamics. In other words, there are many benefits gained by attending sessions that do not last too long – no more than 3 hours' training, where you will simply have to talk and listen.

Offering an innovative tool for supporting talented people, enabling creation, shaping and supporting a high-potential talent pool

Collective mentoring is a very effective tool for detecting, following, retaining, training and engaging talented and high-potential people in your organisation, by enabling them to be visible, trained and heard, to learn and grow through contact with their peers – the other mentees – and with several mentors. You can innovate by offering them the chance to experiment with a unique support methodology. Work on your employer brand. Offer a quality support tool that is new to the market!

Promoting a policy and culture of diversity

Collective mentoring facilitates integration of cultures and professional practices as it breaks down barriers between professional disciplines, positions and professional practices in a very positive manner for the benefit of your entire organisation giving a global perspective, and valuing collaboration.

Focus on a collective mentoring session

Sit in on a collective mentoring session (Figure 4.6). You can see and evaluate for yourself how rich and powerful a collective mentoring session can be. You just have to try it out.

A collective mentoring session creates a multi-dimensional dynamic that gathers within the same timeframe individuals and one group. They will all work together on different and specific subjects that are 'hot' topics for your organisation. Individuals will also work on what it means to them to be one person within a given group and how they can contribute to it. Your company will also work on how to find efficient ways to organise and to lead groups, and what their goals and purposes should be.

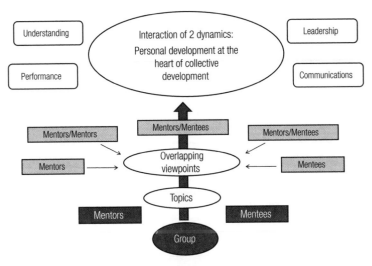

Figure 4.6 Mapping a collective mentoring session

brilliant exercise

What does your team currently need?

1 _____

2 _____

3 _____

4 _____

5 _____

Do you think that mentoring could help you to realise these objectives?

_____

_____

_____

_____

_____

What would you choose?

☐ Individual mentoring

For which objectives?

_____

_____

_____

_____

☐ Collective mentoring

For which objectives?

_____

_____

_____

_____

brilliant recap

In this chapter, these are the main points to consider when trying to decide whether to join an individual mentoring programme or a collective mentoring programme; or when you would like to implement one of the two within your company.

1 As a mentee, an individual mentoring programme will help you build your professional career from a new and enriching perspective. Having a mentor will encourage you to achieve your objectives and set up effective action plans. Before engaging in a mentoring programme, check your needs and motivation by asking yourself a few key questions.

2 As a mentor, you will become a role model, capitalising on your professional experience and expertise. Being a mentor will give you a unique opportunity to share all you have learnt during your

career, and to increase your awareness of your added value within your company. Experiencing mentoring management will give you the opportunity to complete and perfect your skills as manager.

3 An individual mentoring relationship creates an augmented reality where mentors and mentees watch themselves working and learning from their experience and their career path.

4 The aim of an individual mentoring programme is to allow mentors and mentees to benefit from the mentoring relationship to discover practical solutions to a wide range of situations they meet; and to improve and reinforce their respective skills.

5 Collective mentoring organises sessions that involve several mentors and mentees who together will address topics chosen by your company – most of the time your company will audit your and its needs regarding the topics to be covered.

6 There are two dynamics within collective mentoring programmes: the mentor dynamic defined by the input and analysis line, and the mentee dynamic defined by the questioning and hypothesis line.

7 Collective mentoring offers personal collective support. Mentors and mentees interact with several mentors and several mentees.

8 As mentees, your demands will be completed by the questioning of other mentees and deepened by the contributions of a panel of mentors.

9 The mentee's individual growth is amplified by the dynamic and the leadership of a group that learns to behave as an effective team.

10 Mentors and mentees will learn to be themselves within the mentoring group and how to contribute to it.

11 Your company will use innovative ways to lead groups and to find solutions to the challenges and issues it faces.

12 You need the expertise of an external facilitator to lead, guide and train the mentoring group. The external facilitator will report to your company the contents and the results of the collective mentoring session.

Notes

[1] The subjects covered in collective mentoring may be basically the same as those addressed in individual mentoring. One of the main differences is the possibility of covering more business and organisational issues in a collective mentoring session, as well as addressing the professional and personal development of the participants.

[2] Intrapreneurial skills are very often required today and managers are looking for them. They include the capacity to act and to be involved as an entrepreneur within the company you are working for.

PART 2

The how
of mentoring

CHAPTER 5

What makes an effective mentor: success factors, attitudes and communication

How this chapter will help you

To be an effective mentor, you need to be trained. This chapter will help you understand the position to adopt to succeed as a mentor. You will learn your key success factors.

We have looked at the role of mentors in a collective mentoring programme. So we will now look at the role and attitude of mentors in an individual programme. Let us first consider all the participants in a mentoring programme and the relational dynamic established among these various participants.

Relational dynamic of participants in an individual mentoring programme

This dynamic creates a system that generates and develops collective intelligence by establishing a personal mentoring relationship between mentor and mentee. The individual mentoring programmes are based on the formation of pairs of mentors and mentees.

There are four main participants in an individual mentoring programme:

1 *The mentors*: They contribute to the professional growth and development of potential in the mentees, in a context that is both formal – structured within the process methodology, and informal – as there is no hierarchical aspect intrinsic to the mentoring relationship.

2 *The mentees*: Within the mentoring relationship, they receive support that enables them to develop both professionally and personally in an informal, non-hierarchical framework of mutual goodwill.

3 *Internal expert facilitators*: They contribute to the qualification, definition, support, mediation and evaluation of the mentoring programme jointly with the external expert facilitator. They attend to the improvement of this support device and the means to ensure its durability, in accordance with the values of the organisation. They are not the same as HR career advisers, and do not replace this function. They form a mentoring steering committee.

4 *The external expert facilitator*: This person provides expertise and experience to implement, launch, inspire, evaluate and run the entire mentoring programme. The external sponsor acts as mediator and facilitator throughout the programme, working closely with the internal mentoring steering committee.

Are mentors and mentees bound by a contract?

The various participants in the programme are linked, in the first instance, by a specific commitment on the part of the stakeholders, formalised by an ethics charter governing the relationship, the interaction and roles of each person. This sets out the essential, irreducible prerequisites for a commitment as mentor, mentee or expert facilitator in the programme. As well as the ethics charter, the contractual relationship may take the form of a bilateral mentor–mentee contract and a trilateral mentor–mentee–organisation contract.

The ethics charter for the mentor has a binding force. In agreeing to be mentor, you recognise:

- your commitment to keeping confidential the discussions within the mentoring relationship;
- your commitment to the mentoring programme;
- shared responsibility within the mentoring relationship;
- respect and intellectual honesty;
- openness and flexibility;
- sharing and goodwill in the discussions;
- respect for the mentee's personality: being non-judgemental and not seeking to impose your own point of view.

If these points are not recognised before the programme begins, the mentor will be unable to maintain their position, or act effectively. There will be a negative impact on the mentoring relationship. Indeed, as a mentor, you need to take time to reflect on the terms defining your prior commitment to the programme.

What are your tasks as a mentor?

First of all, you must ask yourself a number of questions before signing the code of conduct, marking the start of the programme. It is important that you carry out a personal debriefing session.

brilliant exercise

Checklist of my expectations for my role as mentor:

☐ What, in my view, does it mean 'to be a mentor'?

_____

_____ ▶

- [ ] What ideas come to mind when I think about this word 'mentor'?

_____

_____

- [ ] Considering myself in the role of mentor, how do I see myself?

_____

_____

- [ ] Who has been a positive mentor for me in my own career?

_____

_____

- [ ] What do I think that the mentee will expect from me in my role as mentor?

_____

_____

- [ ] What am I expecting of my role as mentor?

_____

_____

- [ ] What are my values as a mentor?

_____

_____

- [ ] What am I expecting of the mentoring programme?

_____

_____

- [ ] As mentor, how do I envisage the mentoring relationship?

_____

_____

- [ ] How far and on what issues am I prepared to interact?

_____

_____

Main characteristics and functions of the mentor

- Offers an open relationship of goodwill.
- Acts as role-model, sharing all their experience and career history.
- Accepts, validates and clarifies the mentee's own perceptions of their professional situation.
- Gives support and encouragement.
- Enables confidence-building.
- Contributes to the development of the mentee's professional and behavioural skills.
- Challenges the mentee on their choices, decisions, directions and ways of thinking.
- Supports the mentee through change.

Your mentor's undertakings: to support the mentee in their objectives

Your mentor's attitude

You will be committed to the relationship and will do your best to maintain your level of commitment. Sign the ethics charter and the contracts concerned while understanding your own level of commitment. Respect the mentee's personality. Neither judge nor seek to impose your point of view. Take account of the mentee's personality: their world-view, values, personal analysis of situations that they want to discuss with you.

Be available, in a positive spirit. Be generous with yourself, within proper limits, as defined before beginning the programme. Show empathy and create a relationship of trust. Develop and use your empathy, this specific ability to identify with the other person, to put yourself in your mentee's place, seeking to understand them better and adapt your support accordingly. This will help you to meet their needs as mentee and the professional objectives expressed at the beginning of the programme. Never forget that empathy and confidentiality are key factors that establish and build trust.

Encourage a framework of goodwill for the mentoring relationship. Create a framework that encourages free exchange and nurtures trust. Be authentic and speak the truth. Be yourself. This is an irreducible parameter, intrinsic to the success of the mentoring programme. The more truthful your words, the greater the impact of what you deliver. Value the contribution to the success of another professional. Recognise the value of what you bring to your mentee, at the professional level as well as in terms of personal development. Be aware of the significance of your support, and how it mirrors your own experience. Ask yourself how to use it outside the mentoring relationship in your everyday life (with those you speak to, with your teams); in other words, how to transfer this teaching to yourself in managing your colleagues and how it can feed your own leadership skills. Value your contribution in your commitment and involvement, and in helping another person to succeed and develop. It is a satisfying position to hold.

Value the trust of your mentee. Consider and prize the credit the mentee gives you, the 'contract of trust' between you, the positive assumption your mentee will take in accepting all the elements they will exchange with you.

Be careful! Do not behave like a line manager. Avoid behaviour and speech that will put you in a superior position over your mentee. This would break the contract of trust and would be contrary to the preliminary code of conduct agreed before you undertook the programme.

 **tip**

The mentoring relationship is primarily a balanced symmetry, maintaining equality between the participants. Mentors and mentees just make different contributions.

Focus on sharing experience

Help the mentee to develop their own professional and/or personal plan. Take part in drawing up and planning your mentee's professional and personal roadmap, starting from their present situation and proposed objectives. Help the mentee to structure projects and draw upon a realistic, achievable action plan.

Give constructive advice and implement a positive educational process

Make suggestions, recommendations and proposals based on a positive educational process and positive methodology. Find a way of expressing yourself that puts the guidance you offer into a stimulating and encouraging framework.

Listen actively and give effective feedback

Use your listening abilities. Be open to the words of the mentee and 'take care' expressing and delivering your feedback. Your feedback must be necessary, appropriate, realistic, practical, understandable and offered in a positive way. Your main purpose is to enable the mentee to nurture their career path and reflections, to make progress, moving forward and establishing a firm basis in the wider field of their actions.

Speak about yourself and your own path from every angle

Talk about all the factors that have contributed to your own professional career path, to get you where you are today. The closer you approach your own individual sense of authenticity, accuracy and reality of your experiences, the better model you will be for your mentee.

 **tip**

It is only really possible to convey the reality of what is a true and lived experience.

Share your network and help the mentee to make contacts and nourish a mentoring community

Suggest appropriate contacts that will help the mentee achieve their action plan and construct their own professional road map in line with the objectives proposed to you and which you have discussed with your mentee. Bear in mind that you are not replacing HR in career management. Individual mentoring creates a new type of network within organisations, building new mentoring communities formed of mentors and mentees who meet at different stages of the programme as well as outside it.

Compliance with the programme procedures

Respect the code of confidentiality in discussions. Always confirm with your mentee the framework for discussions. Make explicit the situation of the mentoring relationship between you, with your commitments, your mutual attitudes and the equal balance of your relationship.

Confirm and validate the various stages and the means of achieving the mentee's action plans

Continually review and clarify your mentee's objectives. Establish staging posts with your mentee, using practical tracking sheets to help you. As the programme and the discussions proceed, take time with your mentee to confirm that the means used for successful outcomes to action plans are appropriate, relevant and form effective levers for progress in achieving objectives.

Be very careful not to take risks with your mentee

Carefully attend to the dynamics of the mentoring relationship, ensure that your mentee takes no uncontrolled risks in an attempt to respond too quickly to your proposals and advice, with over-enthusiastic expectations that could lead to a setback greater than the benefits expected at the outset. Explore the reasons, the factors and the resources available that motivate, encourage and enable the passage to action at each decisive stage.

Take your commitment to the mentee up to the wire

Maintain the quality of your commitment, your attitude as mentor, your availability through to the end and the ethical framework.

Know how to leave the mentoring programme

Accept the fact of leaving your position as mentor and leaving the programme. Capitalise on the benefits acquired during the programme, and translate them to your own professional field (Figure 5.1). Inspire other mentors!

Benefits of mentoring for the mentor

Have the satisfaction of sharing your experiences, skills and expertise. Become a role-model by passing on experience, sharing your career path and talking about it

Be an example personified and inspire others. Learn to help! Mentoring is a rewarding experience for mentors. You will

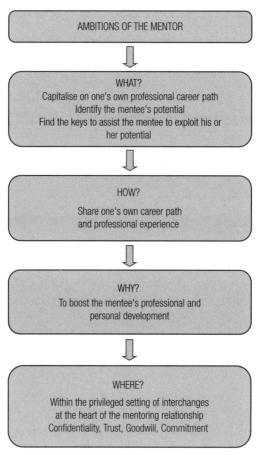

Figure 5.1 The mentor's ambitions within the mentoring relationship

have the opportunity to share the many professional situations you have faced during your career. You will talk about your career path. Your successes and problems provide an opportunity to step back for an overview of the map of your own experience. It is also a way of making the discussions with your mentee meaningful, while also giving meaning to everything the mentee brings to your meetings.

It is an extremely positive and enhancing experience for mentors to take up the thread of their experience, explain what has been gained, with the objectives and methods used, and the means and resources available or lacking.

 **tip**

Becoming a mentor is a unique and positive way of acting as a role-model for yourself.

Contribute to the growth and development of potential in other professionals

Bring value by helping another professional to develop. As a mentor, you will get involved and take part in the success of another member of the organisation, by providing help and qualitative monitoring, within a relationship with no managerial challenge. The mentoring relationship is essentially collaborative within a timeframe that values transfer between individuals of know-how-to-do and know-how-to-be within a professional environment.

Develop your capacity to pass on the company's values proactively

With your experience you will take an active part in diffusing the values and culture of your organisation, helping mentees to understand and assimilate them. Your investment in the organisation's mentoring programme also increases your own visibility.

Understand the diverse career paths, types of individuals, intergenerational relationship. Enrich your professional and human life experience

Mentoring people on different career paths and managerial levels, people of different ages, genders and cultures, whose own functions are not necessarily part of your own immediate field, invites you to experience diversity. It will challenge your own way of thinking and enrich your vision of the world of work and of your company as well.

Access another aspect of your organisation, its members and its different jobs and positions

Being a mentor broadens and enriches your perception and vision of the field, and the way your organisation works: its practices, functions, challenges and the people involved. This new knowledge has positive consequences for you in your own practices (process, management, leadership, forward planning and innovation, performance management).

Escape everyday pressures to listen and be aware

The time devoted to meetings and discussions with your mentee will give you the freedom to step aside from your daily life and routine – however busy and packed it might be. You can spend time in another professional setting, devoted to a rich, non-confrontational relationship, beneficial and meaningful for both you and your mentee, and which will enhance your well-being. Allow yourself to devote this time to yourself, specifically through giving your time to another professional.

Develop communication skills (active listening, questioning), training skills (attitude, educational) and management/ mentoring (feedback)

Enrich your leadership by offering inspirational guidance. The position of mentor will give you the opportunity to perfect specific communication skills, and to continue to develop all your professional skills as you support your colleagues. By mentoring, you will demonstrate 'inspiring' leadership and educational abilities: open-mindedness, exemplary authenticity in discussions, quality of listening, constructive feedback and art of inspirational Socratic questioning. You are a positive influence. You guide, suggest and give ideas. You support and frame the intrinsic modifications suggested by the interviews with your mentees in terms of implementing action plans and reflection on experience. You experience the 'meta' position in the etymological meaning of the term – speaking about your experience from within your experience. In other words, talking about yourself will give you an overview of yourself that you will then pass on to your mentee. You will take a step back from your routine and take a more measured look at what is happening around you and at what you are doing when you work.

Strengthen all your strong points further

Your experience as mentor will help you strengthen all your strong points, that you will then share during your discussions and within your dialogues (e.g. communication, negotiation, leadership, management, networking, business uses) to put your whole career into perspective.

Help to create a new network, integrating and animating a mentoring community

With the mentees you contribute to the creation and enthusing of a new type of network within your organisation: a mentoring community based on openness, innovation and cooperation. Continue to integrate and enliven this community after the programme, as a way of prolonging the discussions and the benefits from the initial support process.

Your key factors to succeed as a mentor

How many boxes can you tick immediately?

☐ Know yourself.

☐ Be patient.

☐ Take an interest in the personal development of others.

☐ Learn how to challenge the mentee's perceptions.

- ☐ Focus on achieving the mentee's objectives.
- ☐ Evaluate progress objectively.
- ☐ Give constructive feedback.
- ☐ Establish and guarantee the context of the relationship.
- ☐ Provide support.
- ☐ Develop active, quality listening.
- ☐ Engage.
- ☐ Share.
- ☐ Be caring.
- ☐ Be tolerant.
- ☐ Demonstrate flexibility.
- ☐ Have an open mind.

▶ brilliant exercise

Identify five characteristics you recognise in yourself

1 _____

_____

2 _____

_____

3 _____

_____

4 _____

_____

5 _____

_____

In what professional contexts do you identify them and put them into practice?

Item 1: context and practices:

_____

_____

Item 2: context and practices:

_____

_____

Item 3: context and practices:

_____

_____

Item 4: context and practices:

_____

_____

Item 5: context and practices:

_____

_____

Focus on recruitment of mentors and mentees

If you want to implement an individual mentoring programme, remember it can take time to recruit mentors within an organisation for several reasons: shortage of potential members because of diary commitments, ignorance of the benefits of mentoring for the organisation or inadequate perception of the mentor's role at a personal level. Question the way in which your personal commitment as mentor may be valued within the organisation. Take care to develop a specific message to communicate about the mentoring programme focused on decision-makers and those who could potentially influence the programme, and the 'natural' allies around them. Then undertake a recruitment campaign for mentors and mentees in two stages, using language that will expand on the roles and benefits of the mentoring process. Distribute the promotional message to the target audience and organise individual interviews based on a table designed around previously defined criteria. These internal interviews will be used to consolidate the choice of profiles in terms of motivations and realistic expectations. The external expert facilitator may contribute to their preparation and their conduct. These interviews will not replace the thorough training that will be carried out at the beginning of the mentoring programme for the mentees.

 **brilliant** recap

In this chapter, these are the main things you need to learn to become an effective mentor:

1   You need first to agree with the mentor's ethics charter, role and attitude. Ask yourself key questions before engaging in a mentoring programme.

2   Do not forget! Becoming a mentor is a great way of acting as a role-model for yourself and for other professionals who need your guidance and your expertise to make the most of their skills and move forward within their companies.

3   As a mentor, you will support your mentees in their objectives and help them extend their networks.

4   You will challenge your mentees. Similarly you will be challenged by your mentees' questioning.

5   You will improve your skills in actively listening and giving high quality feedback.

6   You will focus on sharing experience and lessons learned.

7   You will strengthen your strong points and acquire a clearer view of what remains to be achieved.

8   You will have access to another perception of your company.

9   You will enjoy being part of a professional support process that takes place in a relaxing relationship free of hierarchy.

10 You will escape the day-to-day pressure and routine, making space for the mentoring relationship.

11 You will do your best to remain available when required by the mentoring cycle.

12 You will become a manager-mentor. Value your contribution as manager-mentor inside and outside your organisation/company.

CHAPTER 6

What's
your style?
The essential
mentor;
the manager-
mentor;
the executive
mentor;
the all-inspiring
mentor

How this chapter will help you

Defining your style as mentor will allow you to make a better contribution to the process of mentoring and to be more efficient. This chapter will help you understand the different styles and levels possible and practicable for a mentor.

The ideal mentor practises situational mentoring and, like the mentee, takes part in a process of learning and change in the engagement with the other person. The way you embody the role of mentor classifies your type. The profile of your mentee actually determines your own attitude and level of intervention as mentor. Similarly, your own experience and position within the organisation determine your level of intervention.

Level 1: The essential mentor

This involves creating a mentor–mentee pair between a mentee fairly new to the organisation, and a more experienced mentor. The challenges and needs of the mentee determine the attitude of the mentor, who will deliver the proper level of mentoring.

Table 6.1 will help you discover who you are.

As an essential mentor, your role will be to provide guidance to help the mentee at this stage of their early career. You have more experience in the company than the mentee has. Talking to someone willing to share advice, tips and pitfalls to avoid in a relationship free of hierarchy is a great opportunity for the mentee! It is rewarding and motivating for a young professional. For a mentor, it is an occasion to transmit know-how-to-be and concrete experience.

Table 6.1 The essential mentor

Mentee profile	Essential mentor profile
☐ New to the organisation	☐ Discusses career aspirations
☐ Less than 8 years' experience	☐ Discusses identification of potential
☐ Needs guidance in their career	☐ Facilitates development of
☐ Needs to identify the key skills to be developed	socialisation skills and creating a network
☐ Needs a better understanding of the organisation, its rules and culture	☐ Passes on core values and falls in line with the culture of the organisation
☐ Needs to develop new professional socialising skills and create a network	☐ Suggests ways of improving the skills identified, with a medium- and long-term projected action plan
	☐ Modifies behaviour
	☐ Gives positive, constructive feedback
	☐ Shares know-how and experience
	☐ Advises and guides

Level 2: The manager-mentor

This involves creating a mentor–mentee pair between a young manager in the organisation, and a mentor with proven managerial experience. The challenges and needs of the mentee determine the attitude of the mentor, who will deliver the proper level of mentoring.

Table 6.2 will help you discover who you are.

Table 6.2 The manager-mentor

Mentee profile	Manager-mentor profile
☐ Young manager	☐ Helps in identifying strengths and weaknesses
☐ Around 10 years' experience	
☐ Need to consolidate early professional stages and career steps	☐ Helps in cultivating core competencies, in order to take on new roles within the organisation
☐ Need for feedback that challenges professional practices	☐ Discussions around barriers to career progress and to unlock potential
☐ Need for a better understanding of the dynamic of organisations, reporting and professional practice anchored in good managerial practices	☐ Facilitating confidence and development of know-how-to-be
	☐ Facilitating self-awareness and clear self-knowledge
☐ Need for more effective communication skills	☐ Embodying a role-model. Sharing specific situations involving acting as an exemplar of leadership and management
☐ Need for a better understanding of the challenges and expectations of leadership	☐ Facilitating understanding of leadership
	☐ Challenges and inspires
	☐ Shares stories of success and failure

As a mentee, you are about to take another important step and you need refined, focused guidance. A manager-mentor already has thorough experience in managing teams and peers and knows the key stages in your career path and the key positions to handle. The manager-mentor has a good understanding of business rules and what the company's strategy might be. As a mentor, you will have the opportunity to be more than a manager! Forget hierarchy, evaluation and bonuses.

Experiment with another kind of management that will allow you to remain an efficient manager while relaxing in the mentoring relationship. Mentoring management is a new horizon in which you can express everything you wanted to say about your professional experience and your general knowledge of how companies usually work, which up till now, you have had no opportunity to share in another context.

Level 3: The executive mentor

This involves creating a mentor–mentee pair, formed of a mentee considered to be an experienced manager and a mentor with a profile as director or top manager. The challenges and needs of the mentee determine the attitude of the mentor, who will deliver the proper level of mentoring.

Table 6.3 will help you discover who you are.

The executive mentor is a seasoned manager with strong experience within large organisations. As an executive mentor, you have already had experience in sharing and training managers and peers. You know how to build executive presence, how to find your way in a complex and sometimes tricky environment. Reading business practices and decoding professional environments require experience and guidance. As a mentee, you need an executive mentor to help you embrace new and larger perspectives in your career path. You will talk with your executive mentor about the adjustments required to your current practices. Are you missing something when it comes to understanding what is at stake regarding the new strategy of your company? Is your network still helpful when you need access to key information or to those who have real influence on your company? Are you sure that you are having a significant impact through your deeds and actions? You might also need to look at the decision-making process with fresh eyes.

Table 6.3 The executive mentor

Mentee profile	Executive-mentor profile
☐ Experienced manager	☐ Discusses critical strengths and weaknesses. Professional identity and profiling
☐ Need to share broader perspectives on the business and the organisation	☐ Facilitates future management thinking
☐ Need to share the strategic decision-making processes and risk-taking.	☐ Hones cross-cultural, cross-managerial and cross-functional skills
☐ Need to sharpen the management of colleagues and teams	☐ Explores how to improve managerial and leadership acumen
☐ Need to consolidate leadership style	☐ Facilitates self-assessment, self-appraisal and self-awareness
☐ Need to optimise alliance strategies	☐ Provides expertise and advice on strategic business issues
☐ Need to develop personal branding and a powerful communication style	☐ Delivers high quality feedback
	☐ Capitalises on potential and talents
	☐ Teaches and shares how to master the art of communication
	☐ Sponsors career opportunities, if required

Level 4: The all-inspiring mentor

This involves creating a mentor–mentee pair between a mentee and a mentor recognised for their leadership. The challenges and needs of the mentee determine the attitude of the mentor, who will deliver the proper level of mentoring.

Table 6.4 will help you discover who you are.

Table 6.4 The all-inspiring mentor

Typical mentee profile	All-inspiring mentor profile
☐ Executive manager	☐ Explores strategies that maximise personal and collective performance
☐ Need to move up to the next stage on:	
☐ business strategy	☐ Analyses strategic and relevant case studies
☐ organisational challenges	
☐ governance and vision	☐ Explores show to improve peak performance. 360-degree feedback
☐ management	
☐ leadership and co-leading	☐ Poses thought-provoking questions and problem issues
☐ innovation and forward-planning	
☐ communication	☐ Nourishes and imparts executive vision, leadership and wisdom
☐ leading change	
	☐ Enhances executive and inspiring presence
	☐ Explores how to make the most of emotional intelligence
	☐ Shares how to use an inspiring communication
	☐ Explores how to think outside of the box and how to innovate further
	☐ Explores how to align people and how to gather co-leaders and followers
	☐ Explores how to use agility and how to lead change continuously
	☐ Sponsors career opportunities, if required

As an executive manager, you need to perfect the art of leading and co-leading. For you, that means: how to be a brilliant

co-leader with your leaders, sponsors, allies and mentors, how to inspire co-leaders who will follow you in the way you need it, and how to extend your network in strategic ways. You need to magnify the art of creating a leadership style that is open, inclusive and powerful. You are already able to face challenges linked to topics such as governance, strategy or change management. The all-inspiring mentor is waiting for you! They will discuss the 'why', 'how', 'when' and 'with whom' of all questions you will ask. As an all-inspiring mentor, you will keep inspiring key people within your company. There is one, vital, never-to-be-forgotten point. You cannot succeed alone. Even if you are already a successful executive, you will not keep your position if you are not able to share your 'best of' and your personal methodology: the way you have been trained up to your current level and the way you have been training selected people around you. Because you are inspiring, you need to pass on your ideas, your experience and your vision to people important to you. It is also part of your leadership and your professional fulfilment.

brilliant exercice

1   Where are you in this typology as mentee?

☐ Level 1

☐ Level 2

☐ Level 3

☐ Level 4

2   What thoughts about your career path and current needs does this position arouse?

_____

_____

_____ ▶

3 Would you like to receive input on the following?

☐ professional attitude and management of employability: know-how-to-be and know-how-to-become

☐ position in the organisation: understanding and adapting to the field

☐ operational skills

☐ perception and knowledge of self

☐ self-image and personal branding

☐ management

☐ leadership

☐ decision-making process

☐ risk management

☐ organisational strategy

☐ personal strategy

☐ networks and alliances

☐ vision and foresight

☐ communications

4 Select three topics, and write down why you chose them with regard to your current objectives and professional situation.

☐ Subject 1:

_____

_____

_____

☐ Subject 2:

_____

_____

_____

☐ Subject 3:

_____

_____

_____

5   Where are you in this typology as mentor?

☐ Level 1

☐ Level 2

☐ Level 3

☐ Level 4

6   What thoughts does this position arouse about your career path and your contribution to supporting your colleagues?

_____

_____

_____

7   What would you like to share and pass on?

☐ a methodology for success: self-modelling and learning from failures and successes

☐ a methodology for self-knowledge and building your professional identity

☐ ability to bounce back

☐ ability to move yourself and the organisation forward: lean-in to the future

☐ ability to share available resources and mobilise other necessary resources if needed

☐ ability to manage projects and create new synergies to drive them forward

☐ ability to understand business challenges

☐ ability to mobilise and optimise talents: your own and those of other colleagues and teams   ▶

- ☐ ability to communicate and form alliances
- ☐ ability to take risks
- ☐ ability to take difficult decisions
- ☐ ability to analyse situations encountered and decode different types of professional environments
- ☐ ability to integrate complexity
- ☐ ability to develop and manage cross-cultural environments
- ☐ ability to integrate, adapt and be agile
- ☐ ability to inspire and embody a vision
- ☐ ability to give meaning
- ☐ ability to lead and co-lead
- ☐ ability to remain yourself
- ☐ ability to cope with lack of consensus and not become destabilised
- ☐ ability to use emotional intelligence
- ☐ ability to create favourable ecologies for empowerment, optimisation of skills and energies
- ☐ ability to manage performance and deliver quality feedback that is a real lever for development
- ☐ professional expertise
- ☐ sector expertise

8   Identify the contribution and expertise paths that seem most obvious for your position as mentor:

_____

_____

_____

9   How do you implement them on a daily basis within the scope of your responsibilities with your colleagues and teams?

_____

_____

_____

10 Choose the three lines you would like to work on today to make progress in your position as mentor.

_____

_____

_____

The four levels of the mentoring relationship identified above enable you to target your position more accurately as mentor or mentee. This typology enables better matching between mentors and mentees.

In practice, the match-making can be adapted according to the objectives determined by individual mentoring programmes. A Level 2 mentee may, depending on the programme objectives, be steered towards interacting with a Level 4 mentor. For instance, when raising awareness of decision-making processes and the challenges associated with leadership at the highest level within organisations or for work on the portrayals and constraints associated with managerial functions. The aim here would be to boost performance and development of high-potential young managers. Depending on their respective profiles and requests, the mentees could interact with Level 3 and Level 4 mentors, who have the necessary expertise and availability.

In a collective mentoring context that brings together a pool of mentees and a pool of mentors for collective sessions working together on predetermined subjects, the choice of mentor levels may be more flexible. It will all depend on the subjects chosen beforehand, which will determine the criteria for recruitment and participation of both mentees and mentors in the sessions.

 **brilliant** recap

In this chapter, these are the main points that help you identify your level as a mentor.

1 First of all, a mentor practises situational mentoring.

2 The way you realise and epitomise your role defines your type as mentor; likewise the profile of your mentee influences your level of intervention.

3 There are four styles of being mentor: the essential mentor, the manager-mentor, the executive mentor and the all-inspiring mentor.

4 Be aware of your own style and work on it to reach the next level, so you will be able to improve your expertise as a mentor and to embrace all the possibilities offered by mentoring.

5 Think about all key experiences, the positive momentum and knowledge you would you like to pass on.

6 Recognising your potential level of mentor will facilitate matching with mentees.

7 Don't forget to bring to your daily routine what you have learned as a mentor.

CHAPTER 7

Factors influencing success or failure in the mentoring process

How this chapter will help you

It is vital to bear in mind the factors influencing success or failure of a mentoring programme. This chapter will make it easier to understand a set of parameters you have to consider during the mentoring programme.

Before implementing mentoring programmes, you need to be aware of potential pitfalls to be avoided. Some factors have a negative influence on the mentoring process and can jeopardise a mentoring programme. Generally speaking, these negative factors refer to inadequate understanding of the nature of the mentoring process and the scope of the mentoring process, or inadequate understanding of the role of mentor or mentee in a mentoring programme.

Inadequate understanding of the mentoring process

There could be a mistaken understanding of what mentoring is and is not, leading to unrealistic expectations of the mentoring process and an inadequate involvement in the mentoring journey. We have already described what mentoring is. Let us now explain what it is not. Individual mentoring is not an obligation. Mentors and mentees voluntarily take part in the mentoring programme. Given the quality and nature of the exchanges, involving confidentiality, trust, openness and a positive awareness of change, it is vital for mentors and mentees to volunteer to join the programme. Their mutual commitment and ethical stance are prerequisites.

Mentoring is not a technical relationship focused on the task to be performed. The mentoring relationship is not a training course on a technical subject, like tutoring, although there may be a transfer of skills on particular practices. Above all, mentoring is a situational and relational process, in that you share discussions with your mentor or your mentee on issues found in your respective fields and in your own professional contexts. Mentoring is not a strict and rigid application of the method of use. Although mentoring uses a precise methodology forming the necessary context for the mentoring relationship and a rhythm intrinsic to the progress of the programme, nonetheless the mentoring relationship remains flexible, open to change, and dynamic. It is characterised as being harmonious, balanced, symmetrical, enriching and challenging.

Mentoring is not a guaranteed way of achieving promotion even though mentoring will definitely boost your career; it does this through encouraging and enabling professional and personal development, while creating a new type of network within organisations. This does not mean, however, that it ensures immediate promotion for you when you leave the programme, or even doubles your contacts. Mentoring leads to a positive dynamic of change and progress, the effects of which are felt over different timeframes depending on the objectives you will establish and pursue. As a mentee, you have to accept this dynamic in order to translate it into concrete, long-term actions and maximise the benefits it offers. From that point of view, you yourself are responsible for the degree to which you transform the discussions into action plans.

Mentors and mentees together are equally involved. Their mentoring relationship is not one-way, and does not imply any hierarchy between them. The attitudes and roles of mentors and mentees are aligned on a level with each other in the interchange process. Although the mentors are contributing their expertise to the mentees, and the mentees are requesting clarification, sharpening and realisation of their professional objectives, this does not make mentors superior to mentees. First, within the mentoring programme, as mentors you will act as equals to your mentees, and, second, because you are also learning from the challenges offered by the mentees. This learning process is two-way, even though mentors and mentees are not in the same geographical position in the interchanges.

Mentoring is not the only way to develop. Mentoring is a rich and comprehensive means for professional and personal development. It is unique of its kind, and very popular, contributing high added value to other tools offered by organisations. Mentoring complements other existing methods for support and for professional development, and for managing change.

What about collective mentoring?

Collective mentoring is not a personal forum, a place for self-promotion. Mentors and mentees taking part in collective mentoring sessions do not use this space to promote their personal position within the organisation, but contribute positively and freely to the exchanges in a spirit of sharing and learning. You will gain more with this mind-set and attitude. Collective mentoring addresses subjects chosen prior to the sessions, in order to make a multi-voiced, specific and effective response: a pool of mentees and a pool of mentors who interact. In that sense collective mentoring is not a simple group discussion. Collective mentoring sessions are not places to resolve internal conflicts or to appropriate the discussions to yourself. In other words, they are not the place to settle scores or for self-marketing. It is not the way in which you express yourself that matters, but the content of what is said: authentic, true exchanges representing lived realities, situations encountered, problems for which collective solutions have to be found and new approaches adopted.

Inadequate understanding of the scope of the mentoring process

Mentoring takes place within a particular framework, using a specific methodology. Its effectiveness and power depend on the commitment of the mentors and the mentees, the objectives determined and targeted, as well as the procedures by which the steering committee runs the mentoring programmes.

 **impact**

The mentoring process is applied and carried out at the three levels of performance development described by H. Johnson.[1] Performance to achieve excellence must be developed by:

1 Learning: acquisition of skills, knowledge and understanding.

2 Leading: continual leadership development.

3 Relating: relational, communication and collective development.

The mentoring process activates these three levels in the four main types of mentoring (Table 7.1):

Table 7.1 The four main types of mentoring

1. Career development mentoring	2. Topical mentoring
Learning	Learning
Leading	Leading
Relating	Relating

3. Problem solving	4. Situational mentoring
Learning	Learning
Leading	Leading
Relating	Relating

Mentoring extends its scope to investigation of career development, appraisal and study of particular topics, to searching for new ways of problem-solving both at the global, organisational level and at the personal level, and to analysis of a multitude of professional situations encountered and challenges to be faced. Mentoring covers a wide and specific spectrum of action, making it highly effective.

Inadequate understanding of the role of mentor or mentee in a mentoring programme

In individual mentoring programmes, the steering committee regularly deals with a number of issues it shares with the external expert facilitator. The answers to these questions determine the success of the programme, as well as being prerequisites for the optimisation of its implementation and effective deployment throughout the programme. Do you have in mind organising a mentoring programme because you find it attractive and efficient? Well, you are right!

Before going further, look at 14 essential questions ahead of the mentoring programme launch, covered beforehand by the team formed of the internal facilitators and the external expert facilitator. Try to answer them:

1 To what kind of internal policy does the mentoring programme belong?

2 How are the correct types of mentor and mentee recruited and selected as the programme target in order to respond to the objectives set by the company?

3 How is the mentoring programme discussed and promoted within the company?

4 How is the mentoring process described? To which participants?

5 How is the mentoring programme to be promoted?

6 How is the mentoring programme to be presented to the mentees' managers?

7 How can the mentor and mentee best be involved in the programme?

8 How can their level of commitment be maintained throughout the programme?

9 What is the best framework for the mentoring relationship?

10 How is it possible to ensure the mentoring methodology is applied throughout the programme?

11 What is the best way to respond to the needs of mentors and mentees during the programme?

12 How can their progress as mentor and mentee be encouraged during the programme?

13 How is the effectiveness of the programme evaluated?

14 How are the results to be shared?

Once you have answered these questions, you know whether or not you are ready to implement a mentoring programme. Above all, you know now what you have to do to move forward with mentoring. You have your own checklist.

Recommendations to mentors

Mentors, you will have your own areas of vigilance during the mentoring programme. The steering committee will be there to respond to your requests and help you to optimise your position and create an effective mentoring relationship. For instance, if you do not know how to reformulate your mentee's suggestions; the steering committee will review with you your previous conversations with your mentee. It will help to identify the main ideas expressed by the mentee. You will undertake reformulation and active listening with the steering committee. If you are not sure that you have helped the mentee to clarify their objectives, the steering committee will be there for you too and will help you to reformulate your mentee's initial request. So you can review it in the light of the practical sheet setting out the objectives. The steering committee will remind you how clarification, reconsideration and positive, on-going evaluation of your mentee's objectives together form a tool to manage the mentoring relationship which increases the effectiveness of the process.

Mentors, if you are feeling as if you were only acting as an HR replacement or coach, go and talk to the steering committee! Work with it on the vision of your role. You might explore once again your expectations and needs as mentors. You probably will have to recall the framework of the mentoring relationship as defined with your mentee. Keep in mind the differences between the various roles: HR, coach, manager and your own.

If you have difficulty making the mentee understand that that you are not an HR replacement or coach, at every meeting recall the framework of your mentoring relationship: your respective roles and attitudes, your areas of mutual confidentiality, the ethical charter, methodology, values and objectives of the programme. The steering committee will probably meet with your mentee to clarify the mentoring relationship.

Difficult situations encountered by mentors and recommendations to the steering committee

If the mentor has difficulty finding the right attitude as mentor and their position in interchanges with the mentee, ask the mentor to express their vision of the role, expectations and needs. Ask for specific feedback on the progress of meetings with the mentee, while respecting confidentiality of the discussions. Ask what the mentor needs to make the experience more meaningful.

If the mentor is no longer available to continue the mentoring relationship, question them on the frequency of interchanges with the mentee, on the framework of the relationship validated with the mentee at the first meeting. Remind the mentor of the ethical charter and the value of the commitment. Explore the situation together to determine if the problem is only with the diary. It is always possible to adjust the frequency of meetings with the mentee. If necessary, discuss with the mentee the framework of their relationship. For instance, try to analyse if there has been a malfunction in the mentoring relationship itself. Then, debrief with all members of the mentoring steering committee to propose alternative solutions. Depending on when the problem appeared – the start of the programme, for instance – consider forming a different mentor–mentee pair.

If the mentor wants to leave the programme, ask questions about their situation and feelings. Identify possible causes: diary and availability – overestimating their availability at the start of the programme. The mentor might have problems in identifying their role. The mentor possibly might have underestimated the challenging dimension of the position. The mentee challenges the mentor, with questions and needs, and before each meeting, the mentor also has to prepare the interviews. This dimension, even if it has been explained when introducing the programme and in the mentor training, may have been underestimated by the mentor. If the mentor considers that communication with the mentee is an issue, remind them that the open, free and trusting relationship takes time to establish. Always promote the benefits of mentoring for the mentor. A mismatch between the mentor and the mentee could be a possibility, even if it does not occur very often. Then discuss the situation with other members of the steering committee: debrief with all members to find effective solutions.

Sometimes, after the mentoring process, the mentor no longer wishes to leave the programme. It means that the programme has been successful and achieved its objectives! Nevertheless, learning to finish is an art and shows your sense of responsibility as you know that someone else could benefit from the mentoring programme. So question the mentor about their situation and feelings. Identify possible causes: is it important to transmit, pass on skills and expertise on a larger scale? To promote their own professional journey? Is there a dependency relationship created with the mentee? Gather the views of the mentee in this situation too. Clarify the operating rules for the mentoring programme and emphasise the mentor's expertise. Explore the various options for promoting their experience as mentor. Offer another mentee?

Difficult situations encountered by mentees and recommendations to the steering committee

During the mentoring programme, mentees have their own areas of vigilance as well. The steering committee will be there to respond to their requests and help them to optimise their position and create an effective mentoring relationship.

The mentee may think that the mentor is putting them under pressure and does not feel equal to this. Within the boundaries of confidentiality, ask the mentee for the reasons for these feelings: the factual elements of the situation (words, expressions, attitudes of the mentor) that contribute to this observation. Ask if the mentee has expressed their feelings to the mentor. If yes, what was the mentor's reaction? If not, why not? What deterred the mentee from doing so? Examine how to improve the situation with the mentee. If necessary, review the establishment of their objectives. Help with commenting on the viability and feasibility of these objectives. Discuss with the other members of the steering committee the underlying reasons for the choice of this pairing. It is important to be aware that the creation of the pairs also relies on factors that cannot be controlled, such as mutual appreciation; this is the human factor – unpredictable and uncontrolled by nature. This applies whatever the quality of the matching. Talk to the mentor if necessary.

The mentee may feel unsupported and may believe the mentor is confusing evaluation with support. Question the mentee about the situation. Always gather the facts. Explore what the mentee understands by being 'challenged' and questioned, especially in this context of professional support and guidance. Possibly consider another type of support for the mentee, if their response does not suit the prerequisites of the mentoring programme. Does the mentee really want to progress and develop? Is the mentee absolutely motivated by professional and personal development? Does the mentee agree to be challenged, to review actions, behaviour and ways of thinking? Is the mentee sufficiently prepared to be questioned? Do they appreciate and recognise the mentor's contribution? Truly listen to the mentor? Demonstrate goodwill and patience at all times? Respect the context of the relationship? What is their level of commitment? Talk to the mentor if necessary.

If the mentee wants to leave the programme, question them about the situation and their feelings, within the boundaries of confidentiality of the discussions. Identify possible causes: problems identifying their position as mentee, communicating with the mentor, clarifying objectives and respecting plans of action agreed with the mentor and acting on this. Does the problem come from a mismatch between mentor and mentee? Do not forget to promote the benefits of mentoring for the mentee. Then intervene with the mentor: share the situation with them. Explain clearly the reasons why the mentee is leaving the mentoring programme, if that is the case. Retain the mentor in the role if they are not directly linked to the reasons for the mentee leaving. For instance, if in the end it turns out the mentee needs a different type of support – coaching by a paid professional from outside the organisation, or a more personal, psychological type of support. Even if the mentee was chosen in accordance with the programme conditions, this type of need may emerge from the mentee at the start of the mentoring programme even though they were not necessarily aware of it before. Discuss the situation with other members of the mentoring steering committee.

After the mentoring process, if the mentee no longer wishes to leave the programme, question the mentee about the situation and their feelings. Gather the views of the mentor about this situation as well. Identify possible causes: objectives not achieved, only partially achieved or upgraded. It may be because of an over-dependent relationship created with the mentor. Clarify the operating rules for the mentoring programme. Emphasise the mentee's independence and the gains made. Identify the type of post-programme support, and what specific points require this. Naturally, discuss the situation with other members of the mentoring steering committee.

Among the factors that can have a negative impact on the success of the mentoring programme, the most unpredictable is the failure of the chemistry of the relationship between mentor and mentee, whatever their profiles, commitment to the programme and their skills.

The mentor and mentee do not appreciate each other. As a steering committee, explore the reasons for the situation: the facts that contribute to this observation. Study how to improve the situation if the human factor prevails over the contributions that may be made in terms of expectations, needs, attitudes of mentor and mentee, the framework of discussions, the nature of the mentoring relationship, the mentoring process, mutual benefits and the programme agenda. Check if the 'chemistry' of the relationship really cannot work. If the relationship aspect of the mentoring process is to work, it cannot be feigned, it has to be genuine and positive. Create another mentoring pair if possible. Or put them into the next mentoring programme.

 **exercise**

Understand the success factors properly in order to succeed with the mentoring programme and achieve its objectives!

Key success factors for the mentees

Test yourself and tick the boxes. You might be ready to become a mentee!

☐ Want to know yourself better: identify potential, firmly anchor and develop self-confidence. If you already know your own potential and talents, seek to find new challenges in order to use them. Move forward and help to move the organisation as a whole forward too.

☐ Look for and accept another type of feedback and another way of looking at your know-how-to-do, know-how-to-be and know-how-to-become. And be willing to make progress in how you receive feedback.

☐ Intend to strengthen further the foundation of your professional project.

☐ Seek to capitalise on your errors and their lessons.

☐ Intend to boost your professional development with a full and challenging support tool.

☐ Recognise that the ability to form your network and develop it is a real and necessary skill. Wish to contribute to this collective dimension within the organisation, and to take part in creating a new network by integrating and inspiring a mentoring community.

☐ Wish to develop communication, management or leadership skills from experience in the field and discussions.

☐ Wish to learn how to learn differently.

☐ Seek a different kind of training, from experience in the field.

☐ Want to share mentoring values and develop experience from them.

Key success factors for the mentors

Test yourself and tick the boxes. You might realise that you are already a mentor!

☐ Wish to share your experiences, skills and expertise.

☐ Wish to capitalise on your mistakes while sharing the ability to bounce back and develop.

☐ Wish to become a role-model and develop the 'meta' position: passing on and describing your experience.

☐ Be interested and involved in the development of other professionals.

☐ Wish to pass on the company's values proactively.

☐ Wish to understand the diverse career paths, types of individuals, intergenerational relationship.

☐ Want to enrich the experience of your professional life.

☐ Wish to escape everyday pressures to listen and be aware.

☐ Wish to improve your listening skills and training abilities in management and leadership.

☐ Wish to reinforce all your talents and skills.

☐ Wish to analyse situations in the field, problem areas, challenges of organisations and colleagues in a different way.

☐ Want to enrich your own leadership by inspiring talented people. ▶

☐ Wish to widen your network while sharing experience with other mentors.

☐ Wish to help with the creation of a new network, integrating and animating a mentoring community.

☐ Wish to contribute to the company in another way.

☐ Want to share mentoring values and develop experience from them.

There are key success factors for businesses and organisations as well. You will enhance and increase the positive impact of mentoring if you use mentoring methodology within a specific context, bringing to your company new solutions. Use mentoring to promote solidarity and cooperation, to develop a new means for transmitting the values and culture of your company. Mentoring is an excellent tool for making decision-makers aware of your company's challenges, for example, management, attracting talented people, professional equality, diversity, well-being of staff, life–work balance, flexibility, organising work, innovation, improving productivity, combating stress, innovative management and leadership, etc.

You are looking for other ways of improving motivation and commitment by teams and employees, so take a chance with individual and collective mentoring. These two techniques will provide your company with concrete, immediate results and long-term benefits! You can also mix individual and collective mentoring in the same programme to reinforce their impact and benefits. Remain involved while seeking professional development. With mentoring, you have a new way of making the most of your colleagues and supporting them over the longer term. Implement mentoring within your company if you are still seeking new change management tools, new ways of capitalising on talent and expertise and if you wish to create another type of transverse network in the business: living, internal mentoring communities based on collaboration and goodwill.

 **brilliant** recap

In this chapter, these are the main points to keep in mind when you try to differentiate between coaching, sponsoring and mentoring.

1 Some factors can have a negative influence on the mentoring programme: inadequate understanding of the mentoring process or inadequate understanding of the role of mentor or mentee.

2 The mentoring steering committee works with the external expert to provide support when needed and to discuss difficult situations if they occur.

3 Follow-up and mediation are organised and offered throughout the individual mentoring programme.

4 Mentees and mentors, you need keep in mind your respective key success factors.

5 Mentees and mentors, both of you are responsible for the success of your relationship.

6 Mentees, your objectives should be clearly defined at the beginning of the programme, reviewed, re-evaluated and adjusted regularly throughout the mentoring cycle.

7 Mentors and mentees, ensure that you have established a climate of mutual trust and confidentiality.

8 Mentors and mentees, talk freely to each other about the mentoring relationship.

Note

[1] Harold E. Johnson, *Mentoring for Exceptional Performance* (Griffin Publishing Group; First Edition, 1997).

The step-by-step individual mentoring programme

How this chapter will help you

Implementing an individual mentoring programme requires a defined number of essential stages. Chapter 8 will help you understand each key stage of the mentoring process whether you are a mentor, a mentee or a decision-maker.

Matching the mentor and mentee

The matching of the mentor–mentee pair is an essential phase and key moment in designing the individual mentoring programme. This phase takes place ahead of the programme launch. Let us look at the key stages in the individual mentoring programme (Figure 8.1).

Stage 1 involves validating the content of the programme with the steering committee. This is when the objectives of the programme are determined: the 'why' – the target of the programme, the 'who' – who is the mentoring for? And the 'how'– the means implemented and the resources available. At stage 2, the steering committee begins the process of selecting mentees according to the objectives of the programme set at stage 1, and also starts the recruitment campaign for mentors. Both mentor and mentee applicants are interviewed at this stage. Stage 3 provides training to internal facilitators who are members of the mentoring steering committee. This is vital

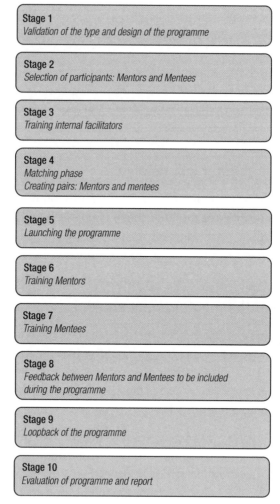

Figure 8.1 Overall implementation of the individual mentoring programme: 10-stage process

for optimum management of the programme. This training is delivered by the external mentoring expert who works closely with the steering committee and drives the key stages of the mentoring programme. The matching phase corresponds to stage 4. This is a fundamental stage, articulated around two axes: requests (those of the mentees) and contributions (those of the mentors). It is important to avoid direct managerial relationships between mentors and mentees. Such a hierarchical link can create a bias, inhibiting free, spontaneous exchanges, especially on the part of the mentee who will feel they are being assessed in the management sense of the word, rather than being supported through the mentoring process. Always consider the profile of participants in the matching process. Determine the needs of the mentees, and help them to clarify their objectives at the outset in the context of the programme. Documents describing the mentoring programme are sent out to mentors and mentees at this stage of the programme, the matching phase is a key stage that requires close attention and investment on the part of the steering committee.

Mentors, you will receive a document to help you target your areas of expertise and contribution towards the mentees. Here are some examples of possible subjects: career guidance; career change; promotion: position + 1; establishing and achieving specific professional objectives; intrapreneurship and entrepreneurship; development of political sense; rules of the game within the professional context; inter-personal relationships (with colleagues, clients, partners); managing competition (internal/external); self-affirmation/self-marketing; developing a professional activity; business unit; organisational strategy; vision and governance; support for change; time and priority management; managing pressure; management; intercultural management; leadership; executive presence; networks; strategies of alliance and strategies of influence; communication; corporate communications; exploring other types of professional activity; life–work balance.

You will be asked to develop the strong points you have identified, and to describe your experiences on your professional journey, in terms of job/skills, positions held and sectors of activity you want to share, all those you feel will contribute the most to the mentee's professional development. It is important that they are guided through an initial reflection on their professional identity and the factors that nurture both their know-how and their know-how-to-be.

Mentees, you will be asked the same type of questions. You will also be asked: what are you looking for within the mentoring relationship and what do you expect of a mentor? What is the ideal profile of a mentor in terms of job/skills, experience or even gender? You may want a male or a female mentor, depending on your own objectives, especially for mentoring programmes whose aim is to improve the gender mix in management teams. Do you believe that a mentor can help you achieve your professional objectives? What initiatives have you taken already to achieve the objectives on which you want to work within the mentoring programme?

Mentors and mentees will both be asked why they want to join the programme and what format they would prefer for their discussions: face-to-face meetings, emails, telephone, web-meetings, etc. The investment they will make in time is very important. They will be asked how much time they believe they can devote to the mentoring programme (frequency, length of discussions, preparation of interviews and achieving the actions for mentees).

 **brilliant** recap

In this chapter, these are the main points you need to address for the matching process between mentors and mentees, when implementing an individual mentoring programme.

1 Learn about mentoring. Be trained by an expert in mentoring.

2 Design your mentoring programme and create a dedicated steering committee.

3   Recruit mentors and mentees after the mentoring programme has been designed.

4   Select the right profiles of the participants in accordance with the mentoring programme objectives, values and ethical charter.

5   Determine mentors' and mentees' contributions, needs and objectives before the matching phase.

6   Avoid direct managerial relationships between mentors and mentees when creating pairs.

7   Provide mentors and mentees with the mentoring booklet.

Training mentees for success

It is essential to train mentees for the mentoring relationship, because of its particular nature, with its symmetrical, give-and-take profile, its non-hierarchical structure. This is unusual and rarely found within organisations. Hence, mentees often perceive the mentor first and foremost as being in a position of authority, delivering knowledge, and therefore as someone with power that they may choose to exert over the mentee. In fact, the mentoring relationship offers something quite different: a place of freedom and goodwill, a positive, useful cooperative structure for mentors and mentees who share responsibility for the success of the mentoring relationship. So at the start of the programme, mentors and mentees need to be trained in how they can own this unique relationship and make their own mark on it, as the mentoring programme progresses. The original character of the mentoring relation-ship thus requires a particular stance in terms of discussions and listening. It is the whole learning process that is at stake, and a mistaken perception of the mentoring relationship could lead the participants to think that there is a natural hierarchical link between the powerful mentor delivering knowledge and the subordinate mentee receiving enlightenment and advice.

The symmetrical balance that makes this mentoring relationship easy and pleasant, with sharing at its heart, is made possible because there is no managerial, hierarchical link. Mentees need to grasp the nature of the transmission process within the mentoring relationship, so that they can properly understand the relationship itself.

Here are some preliminary questions to be put to mentees in training. Do you think that transmission is possible? How does the mentor transmit knowledge and experience? What lessons and how will you retain them from what your mentor has learnt? How can you truly accept and grasp the lived experience of someone else, absorb it and take positive action on it for yourself?

 **brilliant** exercise

To some extent, the other person's experience can seem inaccessible. How can you take it in, and learn from it? This question relates to the educational and training aspect which is at the heart of the mentor-mentee relationship. It is asked in the work of the contemporary German philosopher, Peter Sloterdijk, who locates this issue at the global level of a positive transmission of experiences and lessons that can be drawn from the experience of another person or a group. According to Sloterdijk, we all face an 'almost insoluble problem of transmission'.[1] Society, forced to rely only on its auto-didactic abilities, continuing self-taught, self-trained skills, 'has to put up with forever being condemned to auto-didacticism'.[2] Thus, the major question today is 'to know how intelligence acquired and embodied by those who have learned at their own expense can be passed on to those who have not learned at their own expense'.[3] What is interesting here is that the mentoring relationship challenges this insoluble dilemma by trying to do everything that is positively and practically possible in the format, methodology and support system used, so that the person who has learned something can transmit it under optimal conditions to the person who has not yet had that experience. It gains time for the person and time for the group, the organisations, institutions and society at large.

Training mentees at the start of the programme is a way of demystifying the ideas they have of the role of a mentor, and working on these perceptions to guarantee the framework of the mentoring relationship in future exchanges with the mentors. This work on perceptions takes place through a number of questions that the mentee might ask, starting with questioning about the role of the mentee itself.

▶ brilliant exercise

Checklist of what I think of my future role as mentee and my expectations:

- ☐ What does it mean for me to be a mentee?
- ☐ Considering myself in the role of mentee: how do I see myself?
- ☐ What ideas come to mind when I think about this word 'mentee'?
- ☐ What do I think that the mentor will expect from me in my role as mentee?
- ☐ What am I expecting of my role as mentee?
- ☐ What do I expect of the mentoring programme?
- ☐ What are my values as a mentee?
- ☐ As mentee, how do I envisage the mentoring relationship?
- ☐ How far and on what issues am I prepared to interact and engage in the process?
- ☐ What is the road map of my position today?
- ☐ What do I hope to change and want to achieve? How long will it take?
- ☐ Can mentoring be a positive means to develop my own projects and achieve my objectives? What are the criteria for success?
- ☐ Am I ready to make the investment in this mentoring programme?
- ☐ What seems possible, realistic or unrealistic to me?   ▶

How does that inspire me for my current attitude or my future role as
mentee?

_____

_____

_____

You will be invited to work on your attitude as a mentee in the
course of the training.

As a mentee, you are advised to commit to the relationship and
maintain your level of commitment. Try first of all to understand and evaluate your own level of commitment. Appreciate
your mentor's contribution, commitment and quality. Consider
and give a positive welcome to the elements your mentor shares
with you, within your confidential discussions: lessons learned,
strong points in his or her career, individual feelings, personal
analysis of situations faced, working methods implemented to
resolve problem situations, specific expertise on a subject, and
the people that your mentor suggests you meet. Want to progress: be pro-active in the mentoring relationship and lean into
the future. Recognise your comfort and discomfort zones.

Ask your mentor about what you need most. Absorb as best
you can what they share with you and follow a useful and
beneficial action plan. Demonstrate curiosity and motivation
for a better knowledge of the organisation in which you are
developing your career. Your mentor will help you to do it. Get
involved and try to understand your professional circle better, with its rules and values. Understand the internal culture
differently, as well as what your organisation expects of your
involvement. With your mentor, take another look at what it
allows, at your own commitment, at what you can give to it
and expect of it.

Be open and flexible. Be open-minded towards your mentor. New ideas help you move forward and clarify your objectives. Ideas seen as 'offbeat' or even 'way-out' often turn out to be very useful as a way of understanding your current situation better, and getting a clearer view of the future. Seek and accept feedback and advice. Try to gain positive benefits from the support received from and knowledge shared by your mentor. Ask your mentors for feedback. Welcome ideas, advice, experience shared by your mentors as a source of enrichment, understanding and illumination about your present situation. Remind yourself you are in a relationship of goodwill, that is confidential and completely equal. There is no hierarchy to create an imbalance in the mentoring relationship. Even if your mentor has a contribution to help meet your needs, and you may feel that there is an imbalance in your mutual collaboration, the mentoring relationship still relies on a firm foundation of equality in the interchanges made. Remember that your mentor is benefitting from your questions during the sessions.

Be ready to work on yourself within your professional environment. Accept any problems in order to move forward. Be prepared to be challenged about your habits, your behaviour, your beliefs and analyses, your perceptions about your career, your communication, your managerial practices and your leadership style. The mentoring relationship may overturn your assumptions in that your mentor's fresh approach to what you bring to the mentoring relationship is likely to encourage change and will invite you to reflect on your actions in particular and on yourself in general. By helping you develop both professionally and personally, the mentoring relationship will abound with new resonances. Do not act as a subordinate to your mentor. Your discussions with your mentor will help you to understand the benefits of being yourself within your organisation and to use it as a resource that will help you to achieve your objectives, reinforce your strong points and continue to make progress.

Based on mutual authenticity, free and honest speech on both sides, the mentoring relationship offers you a calm and professionally effective framework in which to work.

You have a unique opportunity for discussion with someone from your organisation who 'wishes you well' in the proper sense of the term, and who is devoted to your interests. Prepare for your meetings and interviews with your mentor to make the most of your discussions. Express your needs, expectations and questions more precisely. You have little space in your diary, and it's shared! Determine the main theme of your mentoring relationship and use practical monitoring sheets to help you. Keep a diary of your discussions for your personal journey. Putting it down in writing is an excellent way of clarifying your thoughts, allowing you to step back, absorb and gather what is best for you. Your personal account is a filter for your conversations with your mentor. You will better know where you are, what you need, the nature of your concerns, the resources and networks to mobilise and what is left to do. Your involvement and dynamism will nurture the symmetry of your relationship and give your mentor material to work with.

Know how to open up in order to make better progress. Agree to share your most important questions and objectives with your mentor. You will be providing an essential driver for the mentoring relationship and give direction to your discussions. You draw the map of your relationship, choosing the landmarks to put on it. So you will evaluate and explore with your mentor what needs to move in order to grow towards your objectives and achieve them.

Respect the confidentiality of the discussions and the framework confirmed. Always confirm with your mentor the framework for discussions. Explain what it means for you to be a mentee in the mentoring relationship. Express your personal perception of your mentor's attitude, restating your mutual commitments in terms of ethics and confidentiality. Confirm the symmetry of your relationship. Identify initial objectives and accept that they will change over time. Ahead of the mentoring programme, define your objectives, the reasons and causes that motivated you to enter the mentoring relationship. Be aware that these objectives will be likely to change during the course of your discussions with your mentor, to your advantage.

Take your commitment to the mentor up to the wire. Maintain the quality of your commitment by remaining involved in the programme, and in particular ensure that you prepare for your interviews with your mentor. Keep available the times and the framework specified by the programme schedule. Regularly review your attitude as mentee in terms of communication, expression and clarification of your requests, monitoring and managing objectives and freedom of feedback and the schedule's issues.

Know how to leave the mentoring programme. Accept that the mentoring programme has come to an end and you have to let go of your position as mentee. You have the means to continue on your own. Capitalise on everything that you have gained during the programme. Continue to explore the areas surveyed and the perspectives opened by the mentoring relationship. Retain this experience, so you can be a mentor in turn!

Mentoring will allow you to know yourself better. The mentor's gaze is a practical incentive to change, as well as an invitation to take the professional and interior journey, nourishing your knowledge of yourself. The mirror effect in your discussions, correspondence, disagreements, investigations, sharing, questioning and certainties will place you in a kind of positive split personality. Your meetings will determine the shape of this. You will change the way you look at yourself. Career path, journey and progress are terms that describe the dynamic of the mentoring relationship and your personal knowledge. You will receive constructive feedback from a professional and you will learn to be helped.

As mentee, you will receive feedback from your mentor in a different way, and from a completely different angle. Your mentor is not your manager, your N+1. The mentor's words to you are not associated with the achievement of objectives in the context of an annual interview for appraisal of your performance. What will be interesting and new for you will be to receive simple feedback, without the backdrop of an evaluation that will directly impact your progress, your bonus or any upgrade. Your mentor is certainly there to help you achieve objectives that relate directly to career progress, but your mentor is not making this type of evaluation. They also place the mentoring relationship in a unique setting for free discussion, yet anchored in the professional landscape and linked to the decoding of the boundaries.

Address various career opportunities more effectively. Your mentor, who knows your organisation better than you do, will be able to share opportunities for professional development previously unknown to you. This will give you the opportunity of discovering other ways of working and growing within your organisation. You will experiment with other possible routes to success. Knowing the culture of your organisation is one of the keys to developing a strategy suitable for the field in which you operate professionally, and to growth within it. Your mentor will support you as you gain knowledge of the rules of the game, and the political acumen you need at work.

With your mentor, you will verify the firm foundation of your professional project. Discussing your professional objectives with your mentor will help you to validate your professional project, to screen your aspirations and plans of action for the future through the authentic and constructive filter of the feedback offered by your mentor. Mentoring is a real career booster. Your mentoring relationship places you in a dynamic to improve your skills according to your planned objectives.[4] Through mentoring, you will increase your communication skills and how you want to receive feedback. As mentee, you will develop specific qualities in clarifying and formalising your demands, in listening, using the art of questioning and knowing how to receive feedback. With the mentors, you help to create and facilitate a new type of network within your organisation: a mentoring community based on openness, innovation and cooperation. Integrate and enliven this community after the programme, as a way of prolonging the discussions and the benefits from the initial mentoring support process.

Do not forget! Your mentor's contribution takes place within a perfectly symmetrical relationship and interactive process.

Keep the relationship symmetrical

You are not a subordinate, and the mentor is your professional 'travelling companion' throughout this programme. Together you will build your conversations around your chosen subjects, and around the mentor's feedback and sharing. Keep in mind that this is a free, non-hierarchical relationship of goodwill. The mentoring relationship is a place devoted to you, with a mentor who 'wishes you well' and is there to help you to achieve your objectives. Be involved, by speaking honestly about your real concerns, doubts, hopes, needs, aspirations and prospects in your career. Share your career path and the way in which your professional road is constructed: its foundations, chances, opportunities, strategies. Give regular feedback to your mentor on the framework and content of discussions. Prepare for your interviews with your mentor, to capitalise on the mentoring relationship and support (deeper analysis of situations explored and mutual enrichment).

Objectives

The objectives offered are keys that will guide you as you progress on your career path. It does not matter what you feel about it! Share your feelings with your mentor even if they seem unrealistic, way-out, confused, unachievable and impossible! Talk about them: putting your objectives formally into words with your mentor is the first effective way of filtering them through the screen of what is possible. Organise them into intermediate objectives. Look ahead and determine the means and resources you need to realise them.

Express your 'professional emotions'

Talk about your ambition, your ability, the power of achievement, competition and competitiveness, your confidence, the impression of sometimes feeling guilty, your paradoxes and contradictions, your discouragements, your strengths, the pleasure of accomplishment and winning in projects, responsibilities, risks and promotion.

During the discussions, define and construct a methodology that will support you after the mentoring process, and allow you to understand better the strategies and behaviours necessary for career success. You are at the heart of action learning. You are learning to learn from reflection and discussion on your own professional experience and that of your mentor.

 **recap**

In this chapter, these are the main points you need to learn as a mentee:

1   Learn how to join a mentoring programme.

2   Make sure that you have understood how unique the mentoring relationship is: symmetrical, free of hierarchy, based on goodwill and sharing.

3 Evaluate your own level of commitment.

4 Regularly monitor your objectives with your mentor.

5 Prepare for your meetings with your mentor.

6 Appreciate your mentor's contribution.

7 Respect the confidentiality of mentoring discussions.

8 Be ready to be challenged and to accept your mentor's feedback.

9 Feel free to speak with your mentor about your objectives, expectations, limits and your professional emotions. Keep the relationship symmetrical.

10 Learn how to leave the programme.

Establishing and maintaining a good mentoring relationship

The mentoring relationship is at the heart of the mentoring programme. The success of the mentoring process is linked to the way the mentoring relationship is built at each key stage of the programme, and is lived by the mentors and mentees. Let us look at the mentoring cycle through one year, which is the average duration of an individual mentoring programme (Figure 8.2 overleaf).

1 The first session: the mentoring contract

The mentoring relationship is basically established in the first two mentoring sessions, when mentors and mentees are meeting together alone, face to face. The first mentoring session is used to anchor the mentoring relationship by a mutual clarification of expectations and attitudes: understanding and agreeing on each other's role. Depending on the programme,

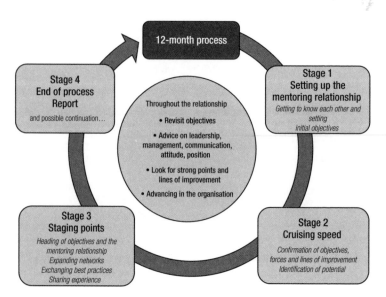

Figure 8.2 Mentoring cycle

a written formal agreement may 'seal' and 'validate' the mentoring contract.

At this first mentoring session, mentors and mentees agree together – formally or informally – their mutual commitments, objectives, attitudes, expectations and boundaries. The main objectives are: making first contact, getting to know each other and establishing the relationship and creating a climate of mutual trust and responsibility.

Take time to meet each other. Discuss both professional and personal subjects, helping to establish an ethical and confidential framework of goodwill, inspiring trust between mentor and mentees. Clearly explain the areas of responsibility intrinsic to the roles and attitudes of each one, as well as realistic expectations.

Define the overall direction and initial objectives and set the heading to which the mentoring relationship will steer.

Mentors should do the following:

- You will state your own objectives in this programme: the professional and even personal reasons that have led you to get involved and commit to this programme. Even if you were introduced to the programme in a plenary meeting and you were trained in the specific character of your position as mentor, you will clearly state at this first meeting your vision of the mentoring relationship. You will talk about what you bring to the relationship, what you expect of your mentee and what your own areas of confidentiality are. You will tell your mentee what you are ready to 'give' in your relationship in terms of time, experiences, soft skills, networks, alliances and possible sponsorship.

- Identify and define your mentee's needs: draw a map! Your role at the start of the mentoring relationship is to help your mentee clarify their own objectives, in order to map future meetings, and at a macro-level establish feasible, realistic steps for an action plan to be deployed at the micro-level. Your mentee's objectives, broken down into a sub-list of objectives, will set out the main themes of the meetings.

Mentees should do the following:

- You will explain your expectations to your mentor and share an initial statement of your professional objectives, in other words, your needs. Bear in mind that your objectives may change during the programme and during your discussions, and may be influenced by specific events on the ground in your organisation. You will also express your own commitment. Prepare and determine your objectives ahead of this first meeting.

Mentors and mentees, agree on the operational framework. Together define the road map for the whole journey, with the frequency of your meetings, meeting places and agendas. Determine the schedule for your meetings and the precise methods for the discussions: monthly, face-to-face meetings, emails, phone calls, Skype. Organise the schedule together, in order to facilitate your meetings and confirm your joint availability. Plan a back-up in case either one of you is unavailable.

Monitoring points

Establish the conditions for a successful relationship. Set the mentoring relationship in a framework of shared responsibility. Determine each person's areas of confidentiality. Mentors: make sure that you identify the consequences of the objectives agreed on your mentee's environment.

 **example**

Mentors and mentees, find below some questions you can discuss together in your first mentoring conversation:

- What are the real-life experiences of each of us?
- Where are we going and why?
- What is the area of expertise in which the mentor would be most effective?
- Does the mentor understand their potential contribution?
- Does the mentee understand what they want, through the formal statement of objectives?
- Have we clarified and established the objectives?
- How can we measure progress for future sessions?

These questions will guide you during your first exchanges as mentor and mentee and will help to move you both into your new roles.

2 The second session: anchoring the mentoring relationship

Repeat the previous process to keep the connecting thread of your discussions and maintain the heading for the objectives. Keep developing your mentoring relationship and build trust. It is vital that trust is firmly anchored in the mentoring relationship.

brilliant tip

The quality of the mentoring relationship is the key to the success of the mentoring programme. Through the methodological framework, personal affinities, learning attitudes and mutual commitment, the mentoring relationship takes shape, based on the trust of the mutual exchanges. The more effective and truthful are the confidence and mutual agreement between mentor and mentee based on their shared availability, the easier it will be for them to adopt the right attitudes. The field is open to a shared, positive influence between mentor and mentee.

Honing the objectives established by the mentee is the priority at the start of this second session. Indeed, initial 'live' evaluation of the objectives stated by the mentee at the first session is desirable. This is used to specify the content of the objectives, to validate and redirect it if necessary. Settle firmly into your position as mentor and mentee. Be comfortable with the prerequisites of the attitude intrinsic to the role of mentor or mentee. Take up the functions of mentor and mentee. Be clear with the framework and ethics of your relationship. Try to listen to each other the best you can. Improve the quality of your listening. Discuss your requests, the needs you expressed and the given elements for your discussion. Remain authentic in discussions. Show goodwill and sincerity. Care about the feedback you deliver and remain available during your conversation.

On this point, remember that shared diary management will give due warning of any restrictions that may emerge on the ground that could affect availability. It is desirable to plan an alternative solution for managing meetings.

Monitoring points

Build trust throughout the mentoring relationship, especially at the initial meetings. Monitor the quality of communication and listening. As mentors, share your experiences to build and reinforce trust in the mentoring relationship. As mentees, take time to listen, to reflect and understand. Dare to express what is unclear.

 **example**

Mentors and mentees, here are some questions you can discuss together in your second mentoring conversation:

- What has happened since the last meeting?
- Do our framework of operation and discussion suit us?
- Have the objectives been adequately and clearly defined?
- What are the next steps to plan?
- What factors will help us move forward?
- What points would hinder us moving forward?
- What are our indicators for success?
- Are we satisfied with the mentoring relationship?

These questions will help you to progress as mentors and as mentees, to move forward and to go ahead in the mentoring programme.

3 The mentoring relationship at cruising speed

After anchoring the relationship in the first two mentoring sessions, it settles into a rhythm for discussions which we call 'cruising speed'. This steady rhythm will be punctuated by staging points allowing peer-interchange and location within the mentoring cycle dynamic. Evaluation of objectives and completion of action plans will occur in different ways at the beginning, middle and end of the programme.

Introduction to mentoring sessions

It is important to repeat the previous process to keep the connecting thread of the discussions and maintain the heading for the objectives. Mentors and mentees, nourish the relationship of trust and goodwill. A quality, trusting relationship embedded in the discussions remains a key factor in the success of the programme, enabling optimum benefit to be gained from the content of the discussions. Hone and review together the objectives established by the mentee.

During the cruising speed stage, the same consistent methodology is applied. You will constantly review the mentee's objectives to respond more closely to their needs. You will constructively assess and evaluate the path travelled. You will be looking forward to the next steps, reflecting on the means and resources to be mobilised in order to establish suitable and effective action plans.

Mentors and mentees, here is a checklist of your exchanges:

- ☐ **Analyse the interpersonal relationship between the two of you:** Does our mentoring relationship suit us? Are we comfortable in our respective roles and attitudes of mentor and mentee?
- ☐ **Debrief on what has happened since the last meeting:** What is the main theme of the interviews, according to the viewpoints of mentor and mentee respectively?
- ☐ **Select and confirm the objectives for the current session:** This involves joint validation of the perception of the 'geographical points', where you are on the mentoring

map. Locate yourself in the ideal position, based on what the mentee has prepared and suggested to the mentor, and also, after validating your mutual perceptions – as in the previous point – based on what happens in the dynamic and content of your discussions.

☐ **Review and if necessary adjust the objectives in the course of the discussion:** Mentors, manage the discussions with a qualitative and open analysis. Take a positive, realistic and effective view of the objectives proposed by your mentee during the meetings. Identify brakes and levers for preparing and building the next stage. Mentees, be honest and available. Bring to your interviews whatever arises from the process and methodology of your discussions, that is, from the main theme of your personal journal. At the same time allow yourself to add a 'plus' originating in your professional field and/or your peripheral enquiries.

☐ **Evaluate the meeting together at the end of the session and set the date for your next meeting:** Manage the content of your interviews to maintain the rhythm of the mentoring relationship. Maintain course on the programme journey.

brilliant tip

Within the framework of the exchanges, allow yourself some 'out of the box' thinking, to be productive in other ways. It is a very creative exercise! Mentors and mentees: Practise offbeat ideas! Also, enjoy exploring the near and far, going from the most conventional to the most unusual. It is a way of scanning the whole range of possibilities and breaking free of our immediate, familiar surroundings to explore, think differently and go further.

4 Staging points on the mentoring journey

The various staging points in the mentoring programmes are vital for the mentors and mentees to catch up on their experience of the programme, and maintain the framework for the dynamic of the discussions. Feedback between mentors and feedback between mentees allows joint sharing of experience, gathering best practices and taking stock within the overall framework of the programme. These moments are vital, and form part of the qualitative methodology of support in the programme. They create mentoring communities, peer relations between mentors and mentees and they encourage discussion with concrete development of collective intelligence.

Mentors and mentees, discuss, share and review your mentoring relationship, your respective objectives and the actions performed. Evaluate your respective attitude as mentor and mentee.

Keep up the momentum! Maintain course on the success factors and indicators and look ahead to the rest of the programme.

Monitoring points

Build trust throughout the mentoring relationship and maintain your commitment to the mentoring relationship. Mentors, be authentic in what you offer for consideration from your own experience and career path.

'I trust him because one day he made a mistake.'

Hagakure

This maxim from Hagakure[5] symbolises the value of authenticity in giving fully of your own experience. That is what your mentee could say about you. They will trust you, not because you were mistaken – that is common enough, ordinary and fairly universal – but because you have admitted that you may be wrong sometimes in your professional career, perhaps in terms of risk management and assessment, decision-making or managerial behaviour, customer or prospective relations, leadership practices, listening, market analysis, alliance strategies, internal or external mobility, promotion, communications, etc.

Mentors, you will tell this to your mentee – to the professional opposite you who is asking you for this – so that they can overcome their own problems of the moment, clarify objectives and needs, find specific answers to questions, reflect on difficult situations encountered and take up their own challenges.

You share this aspect of yourself, this 'hidden' face, visible only to yourself, about your career,[6] at a time when only the right marketing pitch and over-hyped story-telling are the rule. You do it to help another professional understand your experience, on the one hand, and because, on the other, you are committed to the mentoring relationship in order to capitalise on your own career path by passing on your experience, as 'knowledge-broker' and role-model.

Later on in your career, you also succeeded with the support of this individual, personal teaching. The unique originality of an experience cannot be copied. It can only be narrated. In the process of being told, with the feelings, perceptions, hesitations, regrets and satisfaction that go with it, it acquires this educational dimension, and becomes a model and a structured example for teaching. It is also a means to return to the essential simplicity of an experience, without the pressure associated with employability or internal and external competitiveness.

This gives freedom to the words used in an enriching, all-round perspective. In business and organisational cultures, interpersonal communications are governed by the way the hierarchy operates. Communications within the mentoring relationship break down barriers by creating openness and sharing. This can sometimes lead to reticence, through the novelty of the experience and permissiveness seen as positively and/or negatively subversive. At the very least it may be seen as 'uncontrolled', despite being delivered within a regulated framework: the mentoring programme.

Directors and senior managers do not always have the option of opening up and speaking freely with their N-1, N-2, N-3. The novelty of the experience may thus lead to reticence and blockage in cultures with a prevalent hierarchy and demarcation, hence the importance of explaining why confidentiality and open-mindedness form vital prerequisites to joining a mentoring programme. It is important to prepare ahead, making participants aware of the open and transverse culture mentoring creates within a stable environment that is secure because it is confidential.[7]

Mentors should do the following:

- Demonstrate realism, and help your mentee to achieve their plans. Do not discourage your mentee, and provide them with the necessary keys. Your challenge is to give mentees practical tools, paths to follow to help them find their way through their professional map and the means to project a positive image in achieving the objectives set. Your welcoming approach, authentic enlightenment and positive teaching are vital motivating factors for the mentee and for the success of the programme.

Mentees should do the following:

- Stay open and ready to listen. What you are bringing, with your needs, your objectives and your professional life experience, is a challenge to your mentor. Practise and protect the dynamic of the following combination: realism, foresight, motivation and success! Filter this combination through an analysis of your means and resources.

brilliant example

Mentors and mentees, find below some questions you can discuss together at this stage of the programme:

- Do we want to move the content of the sessions on?
- Does the mentee feel they are making progress on the initial objectives, and moving forward?
- Should we adjust the objectives?
- Does the mentor continue to perceive their added value?
- What have we learned so far?
- What do we still have to cover?

These questions will help you to assess and to capitalise on what you have already done and exchanged.

Focus on preparing sessions

Mentees, before each session, prepare for your meeting (face-to-face or remote) in order to make the most of your time together. Send a list beforehand of the main points to cover during the mentoring conversation. This will give your mentors the chance to prepare and do their research on, for instance, details of the jobs and professions within your organisation, or on a particularly sensitive situation that needs some proper time for reflection over and above the easy spontaneity of the discussions. Keep a short written journal of your meetings, in order to filter through the discussions and organise the information received, classify it and transform it into action plans, and create a proper timetable.

How many staging points are there on the mentoring journey?

The staging points set the pace of the mentoring programme, embodying key moments along the way that allow mentors and mentees to check completion of each stage. For instance, the contribution from the mentoring process and the progress achieved are measured against objectives defined at the start of the programme. Comparisons may be drawn in conversations with peers about how the mentoring relationship operates with them, and also with other mentor–mentee pairs. Of course, the attitudes of mentor and mentee need to be evaluated for the dynamic and quality of the mentoring relationship and the quality of communications in the discussions. Check the framework of the mentoring relationship. Regarding the meetings, analyse the number each person expects, the procedures for rescheduling face-to-face meetings, respect by the participants for schedules and their mutual commitment.

So a number of staging points are therefore set during the mentoring programme. These may be structured around three areas: (1) feedback between mentors; (2) feedback between mentees; and (3) multi-way feedback between mentors and mentees. They are intended to be opportunities for sharing and pooling experience on the mentoring programme, and for evaluation: the setting and clarifying of initial objectives agreed in the mentoring contract, clarifying the objectives during the mentoring journey (depending on the rhythm and form of the feedback determined and planned for the programme). They will analyse mentor and mentee objectives planned for the next stage, perception and evaluation of the mentoring relationship and the quality of interviews. The completion of the task schedule and the compliance with the ethical charter will be estimated as well at these times.

These staging points and feedback are also a way of escaping from the daily round. The discussions and deliverables (teaching documents, questionnaires) submitted at each staging point enable mentors and mentees to maintain a certain rhythm in their meetings, despite the pressure of everyday routine.

By encouraging peer-to-peer meetings – between mentors and between mentees – and multi-way meetings (mentors/ mentees), the feedback opportunities offered during the programme develop communities based on cooperation and the mentoring experience. These communities spread the values and the positive educational expertise intrinsic to mentoring, throughout your teams and within your professional circles (promoting individual talents, sharing experiences, seeking solutions, transfer of experience, creating links, networks, trust and recommendations, etc.). This is a time when you can create living, internal mentoring communities based on collaboration and goodwill.

Who leads the staging points?

The staging points are led by the external expert facilitator whose position outside the organisation ensures an unbiased viewpoint and objective neutrality, helping the discussion of ideas, formalising experiences and contributing expertise to the mentoring situation. Members of the steering committee may also be involved. The procedures are defined when designing the programme. The main thing is to avoid any bias that could affect the authentic character of the feedback.

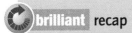 **recap**

In this chapter, these are the main points you need to address when you try to establish a good mentoring relationship over the mentoring cycle.

1   The mentoring relationship is the pillar of the mentoring programme.

2   Mentoring success mainly depends on the quality of the mentoring relationship. Mentors and mentees have to be involved to the same extent in creating a good relationship that fits into the mentoring methodology and requirements.

3   The mentoring relationship follows a cycle with its own specific rhythm and timeline.

4   The first mentoring session between mentor and mentee is dedicated to the mentoring contract: their respective objectives, compliance with the ethical charter and mentoring values, their posture and roles, the framework of their relationship.

5   Anchoring the mentoring relationship on solid ground is the objective of the second meeting between mentor and mentee.

6   After the second session, the mentoring relationship can settle into a regular rhythm called 'cruising speed'. When they meet, mentors and mentees have to debrief on what has happened since their last meeting, confirm objectives for their session, and prepare for the next meeting.

7   Each time they meet, mentors and mentees will analyse their mentoring relationship.

8   Staging points will be organised over the mentoring cycle. These offer mentors and mentees time to share their experience and to evaluate if they are still on the mentoring track.

▶

9   Staging points will be led by the external facilitator - a member of the mentoring steering committee that is composed of people in charge of implementing the mentoring programme within the company and with the external facilitator.

10   The closing meeting is an opportunity to analyse and evaluate the mentoring relationship over the mentoring cycle.

11   When the mentoring process is coming to an end, mentors and mentees can decide whether to keep going in an informal way.

Setting and monitoring effective mentoring objectives

 **brilliant** tip

Sharing objectives is a tool for managing the mentoring relationship.

The concept of setting objectives is fundamental to businesses and organisations, enabling evaluation of your performance with regard to the position you occupy, and your organisation's expectations and needs. Performance management also enables you to advance within the dynamic development of your own career, moving on and making progress while nurturing clear-sighted self-knowledge.

For managers, setting objectives is a complex exercise with a number of key challenges. So in setting objectives, the manager or operational supervisor, whether in a direct, transverse or dotted management role, has to navigate the hazardous line between remaining within the area of what is achievable, circumscribed by the professional boundary, while still being challenging.

The well-known acronym SMART (Specific, Measurable, Achievable, Realistic, Time-bound) exists to cover this risk of imprecision and uncertainty around feasibility, attraction and deployment within a reasonable time. Objectives are at once measurements of your professional value, a means of monitoring your actions as well as acting as qualitative assessments of something more personal, even relating to identity, when they involve objectives for behaviour, and not technical know-how. Hence this concept can be somewhat ambiguous.

In management practice, one golden rule is to evaluate behaviour and not the individuals themselves in order to avoid drifting into a subjective and personal appraisal. The ambiguous character of the evaluation persists, nonetheless, because behaviours above all express and reflect your identity. This is why managing and evaluating behavioural skills is useful, but needs specific training and continuous feedback about your own managerial 'best practices'.

Nowadays, your professional identity is a very strong indicator of your social recognition, a powerful marker for inclusion and a vital factor in our culture and society. It is evident that work affects and constructs our professional selves. The issue of objectives relates to the way in which you as an individual – in all your subjectivity, personality and sensitivity – express yourself through the act of working, and how far your holistic identity can flourish and reveal itself. This duality also encourages us to believe in the complete separation of the 'personal me' from the 'professional me'. The greater the tensions between your 'personal me' and your 'professional me', because the organisation's internal culture requires you to adapt to practices, values and behaviours that are very different from your 'natural me' and 'personal me', the more your resulting professional identity puts pressure on you and generates stress. This has a negative impact on your performance.

↗ brilliant impact

Focus on the importance of evaluation

Performance evaluation is central here, because it involves the issue of recognition. Work has today become a social concept, because it is one way society recognises and sets a value on individuals. Work has become a mark of identity: validating your own appearance in a 'shared world'[8] by a social and collective field – qualifying yourself as a subject through an organised collective group, a company, whose primary aim is production and profit.

In this shared world that you construct through your work, you can question yourself about the very definition of the word 'work'[9] and how – using what criteria – you integrate yourself into society/culture, the business or organisation through this irreducible economic reality. The psychology of work lends work a Heraclitean function. As an individual you are formed and transformed by the activity of work, so that after working, you are no longer the same. Between the Darwinian struggle[10] for recognition and total relationship with work, setting objectives questions the type of 'identity contract' that as an individual you conclude with organisations and management – the way in which you will be managed, be given objectives, administered and in turn will produce organisational results. Sociology today[11] sees the organisation as the 'hard' structure, while management, this famous management,[12] has become a social product able to forge an ideology of society, a way of organising human relationships and regulating action, in other words, the collective management of your own person via mediation of a specific activity: your work.

Good news! Mentoring refreshes the content of this 'identity contract', offering another way to set objectives for your actions and strategies in an effective, welcoming environment, with no hierarchical pressure, where you can develop in a gentler way.

In this sense, objectives meet their own etymology. Objectives are the aim of your desires, your will, effort and action, within a dynamic, a dialectic of the journey. They correspond to the 'objectum',[13] in other words, what stands in front, on its own path.

Let us see how, within the mentoring relationship, away from the stresses and pressure of the hierarchical system, we envisage setting objectives.

- Choose indicators for measuring the mentee's progress, for example, self-assurance, speaking up in meetings, presentation, team management, taking up a position, negotiation, formalising requests, etc.

- Identify obstacles to development and find ways of overcoming them. Find good indicators allowing you to measure actions taken to achieve objectives. Set them according to the goals pursued within the time allocated to the programme. Breaking objectives down into stages and organising tasks help to achieve them. Analyse beforehand any factors that could slow or block achieving the objectives. For instance, you can use the SWOT matrix (Strengths, Weaknesses, Opportunities, Threats) to help you establish a map of potential obstacles. This tool may be found useful in making a qualitative analysis of a situation and in taking strategic decisions.

Define the target and move forward with a sense of positive fulfilment

Always stay open, positive and pragmatic. The universe of the possible constantly overlaps with the universe of the feasible, where the desire for change, the plan, are steadily converted into action. This essential, formal organisation of the target enables priorities and procedures to be set for the optimal deployment of actions required, and the planning of an attractive and realistic schedule.

Avoid objectives that are too vague and broad; it is better to divide them into more modest objectives, that are more specific

Segmentation of actions is the path to excellence and concrete achievement. Separating, listing and adding detail will contribute to achieving success. To make the 'unachievable' achievable, line up the objectives and break them down step by step into individual actions.

Make sure that the objectives you set together are feasible

Being active means being productive. It means favouring a line, a route, constructing a path in the world, a sense of direction to a programme of thought, ideas and desires in order to then make them real and achievable. Effective action first needs you to question the value given to what you want to achieve: your beliefs, your needs, your values, your limitations.

Mentees, ask yourselves:

- What is my request?
- Am I being sufficiently clear?
- What are the reasons driving me to act?
- What are my aims?
- How do I see the next steps?
- What is my motivation?
- What might my limits be?
- What am I risking?

- What am I losing?
- What am I gaining?

Together, identify the means and resources available to achieve your objectives.

Mentees: filter out parasites and toxic elements that could mar completion of your scheduled actions, both within your professional environment and perhaps also in your personal environment. Map out your comfort zone: evaluate the space and degree of risk acceptable to broaden your area of action within the time allowed for the programme, while measuring the consequences intrinsic to your action.

Mentors: support mentees by sharing your professional experience, helping them to develop a methodology for monitoring their actions.

Determine the best means for measuring achievement of objectives, by finding simple indicators

Making complex things simple will help you to validate the clarification of your objectives.

Mentees: pare down a set of projects and ideas to the essentials, following guidelines that will themselves provide the main theme for your actions, assisting deployment. Structure and create organised diagrams.

Make sure that these set objectives remain motivating and form part of the mentees' priorities

Mentors: your role and responsibility are to encourage and facilitate sharing of objectives with your mentee, helping them to realise and finalise a precise description of future actions.

Together, define a completion schedule

Diary management is an integral part of the strategy for achieving objectives. The specific duration allowed for mentoring programmes gives a timeframe for actions, enabling effects and returns to be measured. The schedule allowed for the programmes leaves room to adjust actions continually. During your mentoring conversation, master the art of questioning, applied to objective-setting. Sharing objectives is a way of steering the mentoring relationship, maintaining a course through the dynamic of the mentoring cycle.

Examples of questions for mentors to put to mentees:

- What would you like today?
- What do you want for tomorrow?
- What would your criteria for success be, in measuring achievement of your objectives?
- How will you know that you have achieved your objective? What benefits will you gain?
- Is there an obstacle in your professional and personal environment to achievement of your objective?
- When, how, where and with whom do you want to achieve your objective?
- What means and resources do you have for achieving your objective?
- How and by what means are you going to start?
- Do you need a deadline?
- In your view, are there several ways to achieve this objective?
- You have reached your objective. Stand back and observe the road you have travelled. Describe the route and the stages you needed and what have you learned.

Mentees and objectives

Clarify the type of objective established by mentees at the start of an individual mentoring programme. These will include the following:

- Key concepts: internal network, external network, teams, colleagues, self-knowledge, potential, qualities, visibility, image, affirmation, recognition, communication, charisma, leadership, innovation, progress, inspiration, development, accepting yourself, mobility, understanding, consistency, knowledge of jobs and professions and the group, best practices, rules of the game, strategies, risk-taking, management, foresight, professional situations, recommendations, management cross-cultures, international, training, sharing, feedback.

Have a look at testimonies from mentees who have already attended individual mentoring programme. Read what they say regarding their objectives.

Develop my network: get myself known

- By my line management, by marketing teams.
- By 'consultants' teams.
- By 'press, external communications' teams.
- Benefit from my mentor's network and be recommended.

Learn to develop and maintain a network

- Understand how to create an effective professional network, without taking up too much space in my diary.
- Find ways and means to maintain my internal network.

- Develop my external network and target some strategies to implement, even though I have scarcely enough time to create the internal network.

Know myself better: identify my potential and develop self-confidence

- Take on responsibilities according to my skills and expertise.
- Be identified as having high potential.
- Force myself out of my comfort zones and identify my present discomfort zone more accurately (job and skills, content, management, risk-taking).
- Help myself to affirm myself, to take risks, while having confidence in my own abilities.
- Develop my potential and have more self-confidence: show what I can do.

Get better known

- Develop my visibility.
- Join COMEX (executive committee) and be recognised within the group.
- Get my skills recognised.
- Value myself better and get my skills valued by colleagues.

Improve my self-marketing and perception of my image

- Develop my oral skills.
- Take advice on internal communications.
- Get an outside opinion in order to work on the image I project to my professional contacts.
- Work on my external communications (customers, suppliers).

Develop charisma and leadership

- Increase my self-confidence.
- Express myself freely and confidently.
- Dare to show my potential and name it.
- Form my own leadership style from what I am, the expectations and needs of my organisation.
- Become a model for others and an inspiration.
- Be able to choose my own path and be chosen.

Prepare for mobility: develop my career

- Take advice on mobility within the Group, towards a more strategic, transverse plan.
- Accept insights, ideas, new approaches about my professional direction.
- Reflect on the next position, timing and means to achieve it.
- Deepen my consideration of my professional development and prepare a mobility process for 12–18 months ahead.
- Reflect on mobility: is it a good idea to move, when and in what direction, if the long-term aim is to go for management positions, develop managerial skills?
- Be supported in making the right choices in my mobility plan.
- Look outward for my career direction.

Understand the professional situations I have to face and find the best solutions (strategy, innovation, feedback)

- Get feedback from and share experiences with a mentor familiar with professional issues and best practices.

- Receive constructive feedback on all situations covered during the discussions to broaden my understanding of my job and skills, and my interpersonal relations.
- Understand how to take a risky decision that works: on what methodological and/or informal basis.
- Know how to position myself in any circumstances.
- Develop my strategic sense.
- Create innovation and practise foresight.

Improve my team management skills

- Take the necessary overview of the responsibilities and the means at my disposal, and identify the limits of my/our responsibility towards my teams.
- Put myself in the position of manager: listen to and reassure my teams, motivate them by showing that I share their concerns.
- Clearly convey my messages.
- Set up a positive working method.

Develop my management experience

- Move towards an open management style, managing greater numbers of colleagues.
- Increase my line management experience.
- Discuss intercultural management and the situations I find.
- Improve my transverse management practices in project mode.
- Develop managerial skills guided by a manager with more experience in the organisation and in their lived experience on the ground.

Understand the Group/organisation better and the way it works

- Improve my knowledge of the Group, its structures, key people, strategic projects.
- Understand and analyse relationships and 'power stakes' within the activities.
- Develop my knowledge of other jobs and skills in the Group.
- Find out about other activities and meet other people.
- Come out of the box of my own expertise . . . but to go where?
- Understand the unwritten rules of co-opting.
- Make a place for myself: then how long should I stay there in order to progress?

Improve my professional knowledge and skills

- Discuss the specific practices of my own job with someone more experienced, with no managerial authority over me.

Focus on mentees' objectives halfway through the programme

- Key concepts: internal network, external network, network strategy and mobility, confidence, risk management, visibility, responsibility, operational management, hierarchical management, intercultural management, mobility, support for change, strengthening objectives, capitalise, mentoring results, the mentoring relationship, professional knowledge, Group knowledge, innovation, charisma, leadership, model, talent, potential, sharing, dynamics, solutions, communication.

Have a look at mentees' testimonies halfway through the mentoring programme:

Strengthening network strategy and mobility

I continue to develop my network, especially with management, sales teams and external communications.

My priority remains the long-term development of my internal and external network.

My mid-programme objective is to work more on developing the network in the context of preparing for mobility.

Strengthening self-confidence along with taking up my position

Now I am aware of my qualities and skills, through a 'SWOT'-type reflection and by completely reworking my CV, no longer a sales rep now, I am in a better position to move on. I have to begin a tacit process of internal or external mobility, given that in my present department, there is no chance of upward movement, even in the medium term.

Support from my mentor continues as I take up my position. I remain in this context of support and change management. We share with each other about my optimal position with regard to management, the team and internal clients.

Strengthening self-confidence and visibility

I have to continue to find levers and opportunities to enhance my professional experience, my successes and the projects completed. Gain confidence in myself and my advantages and make myself better known within the Group. It is an on-going process, to refine and consolidate my professional identity.

One of my aims was to learn how to stand out positively, to provoke career opportunities. The objective has been achieved mid-way through the process, which contributed to my change of position.

I benefited from a greater affirmation of my ambitions, and my position within my present team.

Strengthening acceptance of responsibilities

Establishing my legitimacy and becoming important within my team – benefiting from a situation where I temporarily became N+1 to begin to prepare the next step.

Strengthen increased responsibility in management practice

Clarify areas of discomfort in my present job, linked to the job, the role, my own skills and preferences. Identify possible areas for development for taking up a position of responsibility with transverse, more operationally focused team management.

Obtain a more executive-type management position, to lead senior managers and practise line management.

Strengthen my understanding of intercultural management

After these initial exchanges with my mentor, I understood that I was not communicating sufficiently, and that expectations were very different depending on the country where the teams working with me on the same project were based. It was not a skills issue that caused my problem. I had not questioned myself about the 'right aspects' of my managerial practice.

After moving mid-way through the programme

I left financial analysis to join a team of consultants. It is a new team, but above all a complete change of role! I left the solitary position of an analyst enthusiastic about Excel spreadsheets, for a position in the field where teamwork is a key factor. A real paradigm shift. I have many queries and questions as a result, that I want to share with my mentor.

My N+1 declared her intention to move in 2014, and I am identified as her successor. I would therefore like to prepare for this new position and further increase my visibility to prepare for the next stage of my career in marketing. I would like to decide on my career within the Group and I do not want to be simply opportunity-led.

I have taken advantage of a development in my own job by taking on new responsibilities and following the generous advice of my mentor.

Mid-way through, objectives are mainly achieved and just need to be confirmed.

Capitalise on our mentoring relationship

Through the discussions we have had, we are ready at this mid-way point to consider properly together the objectives still to be achieved and to prioritise them, since they are closely interlinked. For the second half of the year, I have also given myself the objective of devoting more time to this mentoring process – a real opportunity! – and to undertake a deeper, personal reflection process, implementing actions identified, especially on creation/maintenance of my network. I will succeed by giving myself 'small' specific actions to take each week to assist these objectives (for instance, schedule a lunch within or outside of the job, get back in touch with xxx). Maintain the regular monthly meetings with my mentor.

This programme was offered to me at a point in my career when I had come out of my confidence zone to address an ambitious personal challenge. During the first few months, my mentor helped me to gain confidence in myself and face the problems inherent in this change of position. I believe I have done this successfully.

Continue to progress and develop within a structured relationship

My mentor and I have a very structured relationship (weekly meetings, planned quarterly, log book updated weekly with progress indicators, etc.). We have worked in the same way since the start, which suits me perfectly and helps me to make steady and effective progress on my objectives.

The experience continues with a shared aim of achieving set objectives and fulfilling a mutually defined action plan, enhanced as time goes by.

Strengthen knowledge of the Group and its jobs and skills

Through the discussions with my mentor, I have gained better insight and knowledge of the jobs and skills in our Group. It has given me other perspectives to guide my career, even beyond the mentoring programme. I have seen how fragmentary was my knowledge of our Group and the opportunities in it! I have had a meeting with HR. I would not have done that before.

Strengthen reflection on innovation

Continue to reflect, with my mentor, on the actions I have implemented in terms of brainstorming and methods for generating creativity within my team. And especially to capitalise on this, and disseminating information more widely around the Group about the actions performed.

Develop charisma and leadership

I forced myself to take the lead on situations which I had prepared with my mentor. I worked with him on my leadership vision, what I have observed around me, models that inspire me and what I hope to achieve. This gave me greater freedom in the field, and greater communication, in step with my objectives and what I am. Not there yet!

My leadership skills are gradually improving especially thanks to the mentor's mentoring. I think I have incorporated the advice given by my mentor into my own behaviour.

Know myself better: identify my potential and develop self-confidence

I have become aware of my abilities and talents, with the help of my mentor. Instead of an ever-lengthening stack of Post-it lists . . . I have written organised lists based on my actions and the skills I know I have. At the outset this was not an easy exercise, but I got into it and I wrote lists that I think were true, others that I passed around my 'safe' circle of colleagues, to get a 360° view. I did that almost as a game with my mentor, but as it has been very effective, I have reviewed my recent professional experience in the light of this work and it has given me a new dynamic. Just what I needed! I am ready to go back to the executive committee!

I have had many discussions with my mentor about his experience as a director. I understand how he steered and managed his own career within a major Group. How he managed to get the best out of chances, opportunities and strategies he developed and sometimes had to abandon them without too much harm being done. I have demystified his position in some way. He seems more accessible, both professionally and as a human being. As a result, I have matured my own ambitions and refined my own career strategy.

Understand the professional situations I have to face and find the best solutions

It is not usually easy to ask for feedback on one's own professional situations, without creating bias with one's manager, colleagues or teams! My discussions with my mentor during the sessions have been a real opportunity. I have got out of my rut! I could talk freely about my perception of situations I have met, that caused problems. I can name the people involved without any consequences. Together we have found solutions that I can apply. His viewpoint has really added to my toolbox, and especially my understanding that I was staying rather isolated within my own boundaries, without a peer or someone entirely sympathetic to whom I could speak. I did not really want a coach. I needed someone who comes from the same field as I do.

Discussions with my mentor helped me move forward in my reflections on my career development and also helped me wriggle out of some very particular situations.

Strengthen my communication skills

Developing my communication practices helped me to be more visible and to get more from daily discussions. I have practised active listening!

Mentors and objectives

Types of objective established by mentors at the start of an individual mentoring programme include:

- Key concepts: confidence, transmission, sharing, enrichment, skills, career, listening, discussion, capitalisation, potential, qualities, network, talent management, cooperation, understanding, neutrality, knowledge of jobs, roles and the Group, exemplarity, inspiration, role-model, contribution, development, challenge, rules of the game and codes, colleagues, efficiency.

Have a look at testimonies from mentors who have already attended individual mentoring programme. Read what they say regarding their objectives:

- Establish trust.
- Sharing experiences, skills.
- Contribute to the growth and development of my mentee.
- Pass on everything that could be useful!
- Being able to give everything I have gained and learned, and pass on all the tips and hints one needs in order to serve my mentee's career and the Group.
- Help a younger woman, offer my own experience.
- Help my mentee in his career development.
- Listen to my mentee to understand him better, as well as his needs and any problems.
- Help my mentee as he progresses in his position and career within the Group.
- Enrich my own professional life.
- Widen my network, explore other environments in the Group.
- Gain experience of cross-communication in the Group, in a collaborative way, without the hierarchical or political constraints.
- Pass on my experience of managing multi-site projects with regional working cultures that vary greatly from one geographical zone to another.
- Give keys for moving to a more open management style and increasing visibility within the Group.
- Discuss the business, its rules and its networks.
- Take time to analyse what works well.
- Help my mentee to achieve his objectives and carry out his projects successfully.
- Listen and discuss, from a neutral standpoint.

- Make my mentee aware of her value and qualities so that she regains confidence in herself.
- Increase understanding of situations through my analysis and experience; reflect and explore situations together through our interacting viewpoints.
- Set an example.
- Be able to act as role-model.
- Assess my own career path.
- Share my communication skills.
- Give opportunities to a young professional so he can achieve and develop his potential and rise in the organisation.
- Challenge my own ways of thinking, my practices. Take a positive approach to other, younger professionals and their expectations.

Focus on mentors' objectives halfway through the programme

- Key concepts: change, career, habits, objectives, support, position, learning, confidence, potential, talent management, skills, organisation, capitalisation, behaviour, qualities, contribution, motivation, enrichment, listening, development, communication, stress management, performance, opportunity, inspiration, authenticity, role-model, discussion, analysis, formulation, feedback, knowledge of jobs and skills and of the Group, ethics, discussion framework, questioning, sharing, transmission, network, transfer, cooperation, management, colleagues, balance, exemplarity, best practices, rules of the game and codes.

Have a look at mentors' testimonies halfway through the mentoring programme:

Strengthen advice on career objectives and acquisition of the 'right reflexes' to manage a career

- Same objectives as at the outset. But the objective here will be to help my mentee in her new position, and ensure it develops as she wishes.
- Give her confidence in herself to manage her own career.
- Give my mentee good habits of review so that he always bears in mind the medium-term or even long-term objectives he has set himself.
- Help my mentee to strengthen the 'good behaviour' each day so that he can maximise his investment on what he learns with me.
- Help my mentee to achieve his career objectives and hold to his plan of action
- Continue to give advice on career management according to his wishes.

Strengthen support in taking up a position

- Support and guide my mentee in his new position, in a new environment.
- Continue to support my mentee in her desire for professional development.
- Help my mentee to take up his position and follow his road map, by giving him confidence.

Strengthen development of self-confidence in your abilities and potential

- Make my mentee aware of his advantages and potential.
- Show my mentee objectively that she has abilities and make her realise her potential; and, in particular, look with her at how she can use it to move to the next stage.

- Once confidence has been established, move on in the specific objectives that the mentee must set for himself and the actions needed to achieve them.

Strengthen progress in professional skills

- Intend to continue with support, helping him progress in his role.

Strengthen communications and improve stress management

- Help him to manage stress, make him take a step back, help him to communicate better.

Strengthen the capacity to identify and seize opportunities

- Help her to be appreciated and be able to seize an opportunity in the same department in the short term.
- Continue to help him grow and put himself forward for positions with major responsibility.
- Continue the work of increasing visibility and communicating about his actions, to be noticed and send the right messages to his line management.
- Support her in her next opportunity.

Strengthen discussion about practices, analysis and role-modelling

- Continue to analyse problem situations and find solutions by sharing my professional experience.
- Stay objective when analysing situations; continue to draw from my experience the key elements that could help my mentee to achieve his objectives.

● Be a source of inspiration for my mentee while continuing to learn about her way of seeing things! Do not hide the cost to myself, and of course what succeeded for me!

Strengthen the quality of feedback and preparing for interviews

● I ask my mentee to send me the points we are going to work on together in order to maintain the quality of my feedback, not to run out of steam in the role of mentor and continue to reflect on my own career path; widen my knowledge of other jobs and skills in the Group; especially when she asks me for solutions about specific cases. This requires time for reflection beforehand. I have no ready answers, but through a comparison with my own experience we work together on getting her requests into perspective.

Maintain the sharing, the framework and the ethics

● Keep up the same level of sharing and trust during out interviews; this helps us to stay within the framework of the programme and its ethic; it is essential so that we can continue to operate as a team.

Strengthen the work of analysis and clarification, in order to improve my questioning skills

● Ensure that I work out theories to help my mentee to find his own solutions in the first place, before I start giving advice.
● Question more deeply.
● Be pro-active with my mentee in formulating and establishing hypotheses and possibilities.

Strengthen the work of formalising and organising

- Ensure that discussion points are properly formulated with my mentee so that I can continue to be of value as a mentor.
- Aim to structure discussions better in the short and medium term, and bear in mind the importance of remaining clear with each other.

Continue to develop the network

- Help my mentee to continue her efforts to create a quality internal network with expert facilitators, key people and allies, and also external networks in her immediate environment: her relations with suppliers or customers.
- Recommend the mentee to some members of my own network. At least start by putting them in touch.

Broaden the narrative experience of the professional career

- Contribute to an alumni group to share my career by telling the story.

Oversee my mentee's ecology

- Ensure that my mentee preserves her equilibrium so she can 'calmly' implement her objectives without pressure!

Continue a consistent internal process

- Apply my own recommendations to myself!

Persist in decoding the rules of the game

- Maintain this continued analytical process in the field, in order to help my mentee understand the rules applied and how to adapt to them. Develop the well-known 'political sense' consisting of many different elements, without always having the words to identify them. It took me years to achieve this myself, stumbling sometimes and making mistakes, especially without guidance! Within our discussions, I continue to provide this role as political guide so that she can implement winning strategies, approach the right people and realise her desire to gain strength and responsibility.

 exercise

Mentees

Which objectives would you like to establish as mentee at the start of the individual mentoring programme?

1 _____

2 _____

3 _____

4 _____

List the actions you have already undertaken to achieve these objectives. For each objective identified, describe what worked, what did not work and what in your view still remains to be done (Table 8.1).

Table 8.1 List of objectives set by mentees at the start of the individual mentoring programme

	What worked	What did not work	What is still to do
Objective 1			
Objective 2			
Objective 3			
Objective 4			

Mentors

Which objectives would you like to establish as mentor at the start of the individual mentoring programme?

1 _____

2 _____

3 _____

4 _____

What would you like to have accomplished at the end of the mentoring programme?

1 _____

2 _____

3 _____

4 _____

 **brilliant** recap

In this chapter, these are the main points you need to address when you try to set and monitor effective mentoring objectives.

1 Establishing and sharing objectives is a tool for managing the mentoring relationship.

2 Use the golden rule of management: evaluate behaviour and not the individual.

3 Mentors: choose the right indicators for analysing your mentee's progress, allowing you to measure actions taken to achieve objectives. Identify obstacles to development and find ways of overcoming them. Use the SWOT and SMART matrix when required.

▶

4   Mentors and mentees:

- Define the target to move forward. Avoid objectives that are too vague and broad. Objectives should remain motivating.

- Divide into objectives that are specific.

- Segment your actions, as it is the path to excellence and concrete achievement.

5   Make sure that the objectives you set together are feasible: identify the means and resources available to achieve your objectives.

6   Make complex things simple to clarify your objectives. Try to find simple indicators to evaluate their feasibility.

7   Together, define a completion schedule. Give a timeframe for actions. Diary management is an integral part of the strategy for achieving objectives.

8   Master the art of questioning applied to objective-setting. Mentees and mentees, ask yourselves the right questions.

Successful mentoring meetings

Obtaining the best from the discussions and exchanges between mentors and mentees needs particular communication techniques that enable better listening and better understanding, thus allowing you to capitalise on the mentoring relationship. Oratory is a skill that serves other skills. If you have not mastered the art of communication, you will not be able to give expression to all your skills and your experience. Mentors, you will not be able to share them and pass them on fully. Mentees, you will not be able to express accurately and properly all of your needs and requests. Good communications carry the content we produce and showing it to advantage in a powerful way.

'One cannot not communicate.'

Paul Watzlawick

This famous assertion by the psychologist Paul Watzlawick reminds us that we are always communicating. Even when we do not want to, we still do it, despite ourselves, using the words we choose, or their explicit absence, the voice we use, our body language, in short all of the verbal, para-verbal and non-verbal cues. This does not mean, of course, that we communicate well, even when we do our best. There is no such thing as perfect communication, and yet communicating is done with or against us, mostly without us noticing.

Why is this? Because we are all different, and this obvious fact is one of the chief factors making the act of communicating so complicated. We do not control all the elements of communication that we express; what we want to say and what we are actually expressing is not always aligned or coherent. We do not entirely control the messages we bear. There is often a gap between what we want to say, and what our interlocutor understands of our message. Similarly there is often a loss – or even a distortion, as with rumour, for instance – in the transmission of information. In terms of communication, we are not infallible.

The transmitter–receiver equation therefore has many unknown variables. There is the preparation stage, not always available, for what we want to formulate, the choice of words, spontaneity, emotion and reactions to be controlled, your own and those of your interlocutor. There is also manipulation, applied to us, or by us to the other person. Manipulation may be defined as a specific way of using communication deliberately and effectively for particular purposes. Every oral communication is dynamic and alive, and in this sense is difficult to grasp. Every communication is multi-factorial and multi-dimensional. We only perceive part of what our interlocutor is saying, and what he or she wishes to say. Our perception takes place through the prism of our own filters, just as our interlocutor receives our messages through the filter of his or her own prisms.

Consider Figure 8.3.

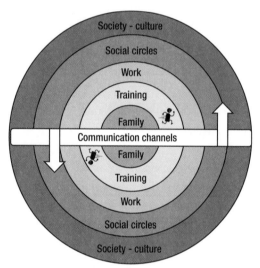

Figure 8.3 Reference frameworks and identity filters

Our professional and personal identity is built from many layers that correspond to the various influences we have received in succession since childhood: our family upbringing, school life, studies, work, social circles and environment in the wider sense – what might be called 'society-culture'. Choices we make in our professional and personal lives largely determine the prism of our perceptions.

We tend to 'lead' the other – the interlocutor – into our own frame of reference when, for instance, we seek to convince them without considering that they do not operate in the same way we do, and do not necessarily share the identical values, needs and way of apprehending the world to our own. And in this respect there is a form of mutuality, in which the other also seeks to 'lead' us – sometimes by force – into their own frame of reference. It is essential, in order to overcome any fruitless ideological confrontation,[14] any negative dialectic, to try to build a neutral channel of communication that is welcoming and constructive, to serve as a common frame of reference throughout the period of discussion and exchange. Communication techniques exist precisely to help us build this common communication channel that encourages quality interaction, conversation and dialogue, and allow us to locate ourselves more easily within the complex territory of communication.

 'The map is not the territory.'

Korzybski[15]

What we see is not reality, but the interpretation of reality filtered through our personal prisms that form the strata of our identity.

In order to succeed in your mentoring meetings, first master the art of communication. Practise the art of active listening all the time!

Advice on the art of active listening

Empty your mind of any bias! Any elements that could distort, divert or deform the words you will hear. Start from scratch, with no preconceptions.

Mentors: concentrate on what is being said to you, without making assumptions about the response you may expect, according to the way you project onto your mentee, from the way you would act in the context of the precise situation to which he or she is exposing you. This does not mean that your experience in this situation is of no use. On the contrary, it will be important for you to share it with your mentee, and that is what they will expect of you. The essential thing is first of all to leave room, leave a specific space for your mentee's perception in the face of their own situation as it is expressed.

Mentees: listen to what your mentor says without prejudging their intentions. Make room for the mentor's words without filtering or making hasty interpretations, without perceiving it as evaluating or judging you. Question what is unclear to you, if necessary.

Mentors and mentees, do not interrupt!

Let the other finish, so as not to miss what is implied. Allow your mentor/mentee to finish what they have to say.

Reword what you have heard, to ensure you have understood the content and thus the meaning

Make sure you have understood: do not hesitate to ask questions to be more specific about what did not seem clear to you. Sum up using other words:

- So what you are saying is . . .
- So, if I have understood you properly . . .

Use silence to show and indicate to your interlocutor that you are listening

Leave breathing space to give both of you the time to assimilate. Silence also allows time for assessing and clarifying what you are preparing to express.

Go back over particular terms

Pick out the key words that seem important to you. Repeat them, incorporating them into your sentences and questions. This is the mirroring technique. You reflect back to your interlocutor words from your conversation that will invite them to develop the point of view, to expand on thoughts and messages they want to convey to you, by clarifying the content of the words used.

Fast facts:

1 Go back over particular terms used.
2 Pick out the key words that seem important to you.
3 Sum up using your mentor's or mentee's own words or other words.
4 Go into more detail to get further with open questions.
5 Adopt an open attitude and retain eye contact to keep the channel of communication open.
6 Encourage conversation!

The art of questioning: a constructive tool for managing discussion

Advice to mentors. Question the current situation and identify the topics for discussion.

To start with, use Quintilian's questioning method:[16] a method of analysing, collecting data and investigating facts that allows relevant questions to be asked and conversations structured. The question set is: *Who? What? How? Where? When? How much? Why?*

 **example**

Table 8.2 will guide you when using Quintilian's questioning method.

Table 8.2 Quintilian's questioning method

Who? Describe the people involved in the situation

Your questions:	Your targets:
What are the roles and functions of the people involved in the situation? Who is affected by what is at stake in the situation? To what extent? What are the explicit or unexpressed objectives?	Responsible individuals, particular players, customers, service providers, colleagues, managers, senior management, etc.

What? Analyse your situation and explore the context

Your questions:	Your targets:
What is it about? What is the status of the situation? How can you describe the situation? What is its context? What are its features? What are the consequences and effects of the situation? What are the risks intrinsic to the situation?	Actions, processes, methods, evaluations, results, performance, careers, behaviour, projects, etc.

Always end the list with the question: why?

Where? Describe the places—e.g. geography and region

Your questions:	Your targets:
Where is this happening and where does it apply? Where did the problem appear? In what places?	Places, premises, distance, services, entities, subsidiaries, means of communication.

Always end the list with the question: why?

When? Organise time and schedule agendas

Your questions:	**Your targets:**
How long has the problem situation existed?	Moments, intervals, frequency,
When did the problem situation appear?	duration, deadlines, time
Does it recur? How often?	management and constraints.
Is the idea of risk associated with timing,	
with schedules?	

Always end the list with the question: why?

How? Describe ways and methods used up to now

Your questions:	**Your targets:**
How did the problem situation arise?	Methods, procedures, working
In what way did it appear?	methods, rules, actions,
Under what conditions and circumstances?	organisations, techniques,
What was done?	means, resources, etc.
Using what methods?	
How were the resources needed	
implemented?	
Using what procedures?	

Always end the list with the question: why?

How much? Quantities used of the relevant elements

Your questions:	**Your targets:**
How is it possible to quantify the elements	Quantities, budgets, payments,
involved that define the situation?	business strategy, managing
	material and human resources.

Always end the list with the question: why?

Why? To end the final analysis of the situation and return to the action plan

Your questions:	**Your targets:**
What are the causes of the situation?	Clarify causes, needs, beliefs,
What were the trigger factors?	personal strategies, agendas
What are the factors that feed into the	and political stakes, ambitions,
situation?	etc.
What are the objectives and purpose of the	
situation?	

▶

This method is very useful to achieve a better understanding of situations encountered in your work arena. Whether you are mentor or mentee, this questionnaire will give you the opportunity to create the big picture of your daily life routine and how to find bespoke solutions to reach your objectives. Before developing and acting on an ambitious action plan, refine your understanding of your working context.

Question the current results

This is the first thing to do to help your mentee to be aware of their situation. You can use questions such as:

● What involvement do you have in the result achieved?

● Who else is responsible, and to what extent?

You can also use the RACI methodology to make your questioning more thorough (Table 8.3).

Table 8.3　A RACI table

Responsible	Who is the guarantor and is responsible for carrying out the task?
Actor and accountable	Who acts depending on the tasks defined? Who is responsible for the tasks defined?
Consulted	Who are the relevant experts who have to be consulted?
Informed	Who are the people who need to be kept up to date with progress?

Question the results and benefits of the situation

● How is the situation satisfactory?

● What are the benefits of the situation as it stands that should be retained?

● What are the elements to be preserved in your present situation?

Question the drawbacks of the situation

- What are the drawbacks of the situation?
- How are these drawbacks a problem for you?
- Could there be difficulties in changing the present situation? For you? For your immediate circle?
- If there is a difficulty, what might this be?

Try to express yourself in a non-prescriptive, neutral and objective way

Put open, non-prescriptive questions:

- What do you think?
- What are you expecting?
- What makes you say that . . . ?
- Who did that . . . ?
- What is your objective?
- How do you feel?
- What happened?
- How did you react?
- How do you hope to . . . ?

Do not answer questions immediately, ask for more information

- Who said to you that . . . ?
- Do you think you have enough information to analyse the situation?
- To whom have you spoken about the situation?
- What do you need to complete your analysis?

If necessary, repeat Quintilian's questioning process and apply it to the elements of your discussion.

Do not imply criticism and do not show annoyance

- Why did you decide that . . . ?
- What were your criteria?
- Why were you so aggressive?
- What is concealed behind your reaction?
- Why don't you try . . . ?
- Tell me what you would like to do.
- Do you not believe me? You seem sceptical when I say . . .

Be specific about your perceptions

- It seems to me . . .
- That makes me think that . . .
- This resonates with me this way . . .
- Is it correct?

Encourage new ideas, a new, alternative point of view

- How do you analyse the situation from this point of view?
- How does the situation seem to you, considering that . . . ?
- Could there be another view of the situation?
- What might be the link between . . . and . . . ?
- What other ways might you deal with the situation?

Make a list of possible options and solutions:

- What could you say about the options you envisage today?
- Have you thought of other approaches?

- Have you imagined any options and intermediate solutions?
- What are the benefits and drawbacks of each of your options?
- Which of your options would give the best result?
- What else could you say?
- What off-beat, even way-out ideas could you come up with on this subject?

Challenge!

- What else now?
- What are the next steps?

Encourage reflection

- What have you learned from this situation?
- From these facts?
- What could be the effects and consequences of . . . ?

Apply a positive influence by questioning: seek to guide without imposing your own point of view

You can use development questions that lead to a more thought-out response:

- In what case?
- For example?
- That means?
- In what sense?
- At what level?

Suggest an opinion, a direction

- You could think about . . .
- Explain why: . . .
- My final argument is . . .

Ask what the person thinks

- What do you think?
- What does that evoke for you?

Avoid the temptation to say, as your first response

- If I were you . . .
- In your place, I would do . . .

Wait while your discussions develop before you give advice in such a direct way.

In your exchanges with your mentees, use the art of list-making to inspire you in leading your discussions. Invite your mentee to create their own lists from the items suggested below. This is a methodological tool that includes the dimensions of foresight, introspection, creativity and self-projection.

Embrace the art of relevant and brilliant lists!

brilliant tip

Examples of possible lists you could ask your mentee to work on:

- List of my objectives, expectations, needs, resources and means.
- List of my limitations.
- List of my most frequent professional emotions.

- List of my allies and my 'enemies'.
- List of what I know about my situation and list of things I do not know about my situation.
- List of my preferred professional situations and list of professional contexts I avoid.
- List of things not to do and list of my actions to carry out.
- List of my areas of uncertainty.
- List of times I have effectively taken risks.
- List of my successful communications and list of situations where I have shown leadership.
- List of times I have made progress and list of times I have learned positive things about myself.
- List of times I have learned things about myself to my own cost and list of key moments when I have changed and adapted my behaviour.
- List of times I have been able to handle competition with my peers and list of times I have handled pressure.
- List of times I have recognised the value of others and list of times my value has been recognised.
- List of my positive impacts on my professional circle: projects, teams, management, colleagues.
- List of my realistic action plans and list of my possibilities.
- List of my dream action plans and list of what I am looking for today.

You could also make your own lists to analyse more thoroughly your own professional experience and to work on your role as mentor as well. As a role-model, you probably already have or you are in the process of developing a clear view of your career path,

▶

> your strengths, your areas of improvement, and have been through all these lists already. But if not, it is better late than never! By becoming a mentor you engage yourself in this kind of reflexion that will be very useful for your current position.

Mentors, ask the mentees, based on these lists, to choose what seems most relevant to them in their professional situation and career path. This will give you routes and lines for improvement on the objectives to explore together, and you will help your mentee to increase awareness of their professional identity. This approach will also give you a more original and less academic approach to the subjects covered, and deepen the dynamic of your discussions. Consider using this exercise as well for a more thorough account of your experience to give to your mentee in the modelling process of transmission.

Examples of topics that the mentees might cover in your mentoring conversation

1 Career management and development: learn to move from qualitative to quantitative

How do you manage your career? This is one of the most common questions from mentees, since it affects fundamental aspects of professional life. This question addresses the way you have built both tangible and intangible capital during your professional career. Intangible capital relies on knowledge, study, training, culture, networks and bonds created and values as well as different forms of interdependent commitment. Tangible capital in turn is constructed on the basis of paid work. Conversion of intangible to tangible capital involves a complex equation. The challenge of a career consists precisely in optimising this conversion of intangible to tangible capital.

Work is often the only way to achieve this. It is important, in optimising career management, to learn how to move from the qualitative to the quantitative. Knowing how to increase your value in order to make progress in your professional life, capitalise on tangible and intangible assets, make actions visible, giving them a shape and an appropriate context, are an integral part of the process of self-development.

In our society today, managing competition, the race for image and the demand for real-time communications in order to be visible, validate and maintain your own position, all make self-development a skill that needs to be mastered in order to be affirmed and recognised within your professional identity. That is why organisational cultures often reflect Darwinian theories so closely: the struggle for position has replaced the struggle for survival.

Self-marketing also develops in response to the management paradigm that obliges you to manage your career and employability yourself. This imposes increased pressure and responsibility on you, and not everyone has the same professional and personal resources to deal with them.

The question of value becomes fundamental, referring to several realities and semantic fields: economic and quantitative notion of value, value and capital – tangible and intangible values, qualitative concepts referring to intrinsic characteristics that give value to you as an individual, a set of criteria allowing actions and thought to be prioritised, the concept of effectiveness and validity, the character of the person estimated, because judged as objectively estimable and the idea of warrior bravery and courage.

If you need to check how much you value yourself, start with the following questions:

- How to measure and evaluate myself?
- Based on what criteria?
- How to estimate my qualities?

- How to make them valued and make them flourish?
- How to develop myself?
- What usefulness, meaning and values to give to my actions?
- Into what circles and value-sharing groups can I enter?

Once you have asked yourself the right questions about your own value, then ask your mentee: how can you transform your qualitative value into a quantitative value? What methods are you going to use to convert your value?

 **exercise**

Suggest an exercise for analysing my own value: who I am, how much I am worth (Table 8.4).

Table 8.4   How much I am worth

I *AM* → I AM WORTH → DEVELOPING A FRAMEWORK OF VALUES
....
....
....
....

I *DO* → I AM WORTH → DEVELOPING A FRAMEWORK OF VALUES
....
....
....
....

What indicators will you use to measure the true conversion value of your worth? My indicators are:

1 ....
2 ....
3 ....

- Are these indicators satisfactory for you?
- How can you improve them?
- Imagine some new criteria for converting your value.
- Design your ideal framework for evaluation: choose the words that match you.
- Find resources and means to adapt your new framework for evaluation to your own contacts and the various landscapes on which you develop.

Optimal career management is achieved by being able to create value for yourself and the company you work for. This also involves knowledge of career opportunities within your organisation, that is, key determining moments to make your professional and added value bear fruit, as you move to another stage in your professional development. It involves understanding how career development progresses: linearity, any breaks, experience in the field and mobility.

In your discussions with your mentees on this vital topic, mentors review major points in your experience and career path, share the different ways you have managed your career in its interaction with your personal life and explain high points and problems encountered, solutions found and implemented. Share how you have built and developed a vision, a personal strategy with regard to 'dangers' and opportunities: how you have built your career path and managed your development.

2 Promotion: how to get promoted?

The issue of promotion, that is the recognition of your work with the direct conversion from qualitative to quantitative value, is a subject the mentee may cover with you.

Mentors, in your discussions with your mentees on this vital topic, share concrete situations: Share the various 'promotion situations' you have experienced. When and how you were promoted. Explain all the internal and external factors that led to you being approached and qualified for promotion. Examples of topics: alliances, network, types of communication, self-publicising strategies, visibility for yourself and your work, risk-taking, etc. Share the circumstances in which you requested promotion: how you explained and formulated your request, the language and negotiation elements. Share situations when you were not promoted, even though you wanted to be. For instance, you did not get the in-house job for which you applied. What did you do? How did you react? How did you recover?

3 Taking up the position: with regard to your new line management, colleagues and peers

Mentors, in your discussions with your mentees on this vital topic, share concrete situations: when taking up a position, decide on the essentials: how to present yourself? With whom to communicate? What messages to give and how to give them? List the key messages and behaviours to adopt towards the management, colleagues and peers. Share times when it was vital to control an excess of emotions, despite the difficulty, that could have had a negative impact on the effort made to enter a new position: panic, anxiety, lack of confidence or fear of being judged and evaluated, stress. Discuss what these situations taught you.

4 Self-confidence and self-affirmation

Self-confidence is an important lever for success. It allows you to dare to move forward, to value your work, to be pro-active and a force to be reckoned with, to be a positive driver for yourself and your circle, and to use your talents and skills to the best advantage. Self-confidence enables you to delegate and

support your colleagues better, to help them grow and progress. It helps create a positive working environment around
you. Someone who has confidence in himself or herself in the
right way – positive and balanced – will tend to gather loyal
people and create stimulating working environments.

Mentors, in your discussions with your mentees on this vital
topic, share concrete situations: what do you do to promote
your results, and to whom? Explain how you have ensured your
results are recognised: the way you have communicated them
upwards and the positive effects for your personal esteem and
the perception you have of yourself. Share when your 'yes' and
your 'no' have had a powerful, major impact. Explain how you
learned to say 'yes' and to say 'no'. If your 'yes' is to have real
value, it is important to know how to say 'no'. Explain how you
have managed your ambition. List situations where you were
challenged by peers, colleagues, your teams, suppliers, customers, originators of orders. Discuss the solutions applied. How do
you identify your allies and the people whom you have not won
over? Share your 'best of' moments when you were affirmed,
with the positive consequences of this. Share your leadership
style: participatory/collaborative/directive/delegating/persua-
sive/situational/inspiring/relational. Discuss the reasons why
you have sometimes modified your leadership style.

In your message to mentees, take account of the various components of interpersonal communication: verbal language (7
per cent), para-verbal language (38 per cent), non-verbal language (55 per cent). This helps you better manage your conversations with your mentee and convey what you want to pass
on to him or her.

5 Leadership and visibility

In your discussions with your mentees on this topic, share
concrete situations:

- How have you increased your credibility?
- How do you nourish your legitimacy?
- How do you develop your force of conviction?
- How do you come to terms with your personality, your natural style?
- How do you make your voice heard?
- How do you affirm yourself?
- How have you asked for the attention of your interlocutors and in what types of situation: meetings of executive committee, board of directors or steering committee?
- Maybe in negotiating contexts?
- What is your influence in your working environment?
- How do you build a team?

Leadership remains a 'hot' topic. You no longer have a choice on this. You need to know what leadership is or might be. There are thousands of books on it but leadership seems to resist any definition. You only can understand what it means through case studies and by close analysis of concrete situations. Otherwise leadership is just a beautiful, exalted word. We all need leaders. Your company needs leaders. You need to know when you have shown leadership and which skills you have used. Leadership is always linked to situations. You cannot always be a leader. It is not a job you apply for. First of all, leadership depends on contexts. In some specific situations, with specific people, you might have shown leadership and you appeared as a true leader, but in other situations you have not shown any leadership. Is this possible? Yes, it is. You still have leadership skills but the possibility of using and expressing them will always depend on the context. That is the reason why talking about very specific situations is the best way to understand what leadership means and is, and to be able to perform as a leader too. And do not blame yourself too much when you do not find the right way to be a leader in your field.

6 Network and enterprise culture

Creating, inspiring and knowing how to use your network, and being able to form good partnerships, are vital elements for career progress. Based on a level of skills, acquired and validated, the network/partnership/alliances/co-opting dimension is vital for making progress in your career and moving aside all the glass ceilings you might find on the way up. It is therefore necessary to learn how to decode the formal and informal rules of the business game, in order to understand better the practices of governance and the internal culture.

Mentors, in your discussions with your mentees on this vital topic, share concrete situations:

● What is the importance of the network?

● Explain in what way the network increases efficiency, improves daily work and helps one develop professionally within the business.

● How did you create your internal and external network?

● How do you use it? What do you do to nurture it and keep it alive?

● List the actions you have implemented to create an effective network.

● List precise situations when the network has helped you, and the points to watch.

● List the vital factors to increase your network and maintain its quality.

● How did you succeed in understanding your professional environment?

● How have you identified the formal and informal rules in your environment? What help have you needed, if any?

● How did you master the rules of your professional environment? What did that do to change your actions, your behaviour and your communications?

The success of meetings between mentors and mentees is linked to the way mentors master the art of communication and of questioning that helps them to be more effective in their discussions and to nurture the mentoring relationship. As mentors, you will be able to listen better so that you can better share all your experiences. As mentees, you will gain a different understanding of the contributions made by the mentors, so you will be able to translate them into action plans that suit your needs and requests more closely.

 **brilliant** recap

In this chapter, these are the main points you need to keep in mind to make mentoring meetings successful:

1   Master the art of questioning to manage your discussions in the best way.

2   Use a wide range of communication techniques like Quintilian's questioning method and the RACI methodology. These techniques will help you build a common communication channel between you, and are a prerequisite for achieving excellent communication and mutual understanding.

3   Identify 'hot' and relevant topics for your mentoring conversations. Even if they do not appear to be among your respective concerns.

Mentors:

1   Use the art of list-making to inspire you in leading your discussions with your mentees. Apply this technique to yourself as well.

2   Don't forget to question the current situation.

3   Question the benefits of the desired situation: ask for more information.

4 Express yourself in a non-prescriptive, neutral and objective way: do not imply criticism.

5 Be specific about your perceptions.

6 Apply positive influence by questioning: seek to guide without imposing your own point of view.

7 Encourage reflection and challenge!

8 Encourage new ideas!

Mentors and mentees, don't forget to transfer to your daily routine, your practices, your colleagues and teams what you have learnt about improving communication in your managerial conversations.

Giving efficient and effective feedback

The quality of the feedback given by mentors to mentees, and by mentees to mentors is vital in terms of the quality and effectiveness of the mentoring relationship. Let us first look at the definition of feedback in the context of a managerial, hierarchical relationship. Feedback is a report made by the manager to a colleague on the latter's words, behaviour and actions, with the aim of influencing future words, behaviour and actions, either to reinforce or to modify them. Feedback may be positive, with the result that the colleague maintains or reinforces his or her way of working. The feedback may be corrective. In this case, the colleague then has to change and improve his or her way of working.

What is successful feedback?

It is, first of all, a state of mind, an interior disposition, a way of communicating content, analysis or evaluation on professional practices. Successful, authentic and honest feedback is intended to encourage talent and talented people or to help the person concerned to progress. Feedback must be factual, delivered regularly, and must be face-to-face. It may be made straight after observing behaviour in everyday situations – 'hot', or it may cover a longer period of work, on achieving objectives, as happens for the annual review.

What is not feedback?

Feedback must never be an attempt to manipulate a colleague. Nor is feedback intended to change the essential nature of a person, an impossible task and one that would never be the aim of a manager. Feedback must not judge either the person or the character, but be focused on the words, behaviour and actions used in the position held. Feedback certainly does not involve any 'settling of accounts' in which a manager risks injuring the colleague and setting up obstacles to their professional relationship.

Why must I give feedback to colleagues?

You already give it unconsciously. Remember what Watzlawick said: you cannot not communicate. It is impossible not to send positive or negative signals to the people around us. That's why it is necessary to organise and prepare your message when possible. When I do not react to a colleague's action, I might imagine I am not giving feedback, and yet even silence is feedback, often interpreted inappropriately.

The feedback I give will help my colleagues to know themselves better and to develop in a dynamic of positive progress and empowerment. I owe my colleagues clear indicators on what is appropriate and inappropriate for the position they fill. Take care, feedback does not necessarily have an immediate effect: it acts over a period, through gradual adjustments, modifications to words, behaviour and actions. Changes need time to be firmly established and become new habits and new practices. The send-receive feedback control loop is used to deliver feedback (Figure 8.4).

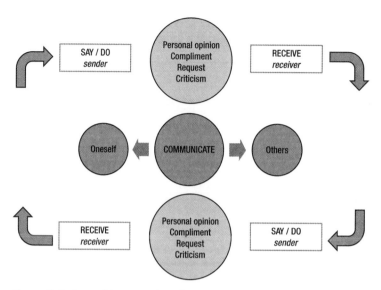

Figure 8.4 Control loop: send-receive

Feedback methodology

State the constructive nature of your feedback. If your feedback is not intended to be constructive, do not mention it. Focus on the state of mind of the person receiving your feedback. Read this example of positive feedback:

I really appreciated the way you conducted the meeting. You demonstrated the ability to synthesise, and your presentation really moved the subject forward . . .

Here is an example of corrective feedback:

I think it would be helpful to discuss the way you speak to customers when we are in a sales meeting. As you know, customer satisfaction is part of our core business.

Give your feedback

Choose the right moment. Be brief and clear, and adopt a constructive tone. Take care with the form of your feedback, how it is delivered, as this should serve the content. Be respectful, honest and authentic. Stay descriptive, factual and objective, do not moralise. Give examples to illustrate your comments. Share what you feel.

Read this example of positive feedback:

I really appreciated the way you helped with this project. I know it's not your job to help with this kind of activity, and I'd like to thank you for that.

Here is an example of corrective feedback:

I noticed that you sometimes speak a bit sharply when a customer asks questions during our meeting. I'm afraid they might be upset by this, and go elsewhere next time they have a contract to offer.

Check understanding

Check you have been clear and the real message was properly understood as it should be. Give your interlocutor the chance to respond, and listen to what they say. Be patient and persevere because they may not react immediately and spontaneously to your comments. Listen to the other person's point of view at all costs without interrupting or trying to convince them. Repeat if necessary and give time to respond. Ask the other person to describe experiences with which they are satisfied. Explore:

- What do you think about what I have said?
- I would really like to know what you think about this situation.

Reinforce. Suggest. Request

Help the person to find their own solutions. Give your own advice and suggestions to complement theirs, being as specific, factual and constructive as possible. Suggest without forcing. Look ahead: work out a plan of action with your interlocutor to help reinforce or modify the behaviour. See these examples:

- What other ways might there be to respond to questions from our customers when we are in sales meetings?
- Would you agree to discuss other possible ways of conducting our meetings with our customers?

Sum up and express your support

Summarise the discussion and the resulting agreement. Let the other person know that you appreciate their open-mindedness and that they have your full support in implementing the actions you have agreed and confirmed together.

Read this example of positive feedback:

Thank you again. You understood I needed help (even though I didn't ask for it) and you helped me to avoid spending the whole day on this file. You showed a real sense of teamwork and I am pleased that we make a real team. Continue like that.

Here is an example of corrective feedback:

So, you agree to change the way you respond to customers' questions when we are in a meeting. Thank you for having accepted my comments and changed your way of doing things. I am sure you will quickly see the benefits. You can rely on my support.

Send messages in the first person singular

One way of giving feedback involves using a message in the first person singular. This kind of message describes the way you feel as a result of the behaviour of the other person, and its effect on yourself. The benefits of feedback given in the first person: your statement is direct; the defensive nature of the situation is reduced. You are claiming responsibility for your own feelings and reactions. You clarify the reason why it is important for your interlocutor to change their behaviour. You clearly state the consequences and benefits of the desired change.

The drawbacks of feedback given in the first person: you have to think about what you are going to say, and choose your words carefully. Given in the first person, your words can have a very powerful impact, even if you choose them carefully. Bear in mind that it is sometimes hard to identify other people's feelings. Look at Table 8.5.

This will give you the logic and the possible thread of feedback during your mentoring conversation. It is one way of practising the DESC technique, one of the best-known tools in management communications, for giving feedback, refocusing, and when necessary, giving difficult messages. The DESC technique consists of the following stages:

1 Describe the situation.

2 Express your own point of view on the consequences of the situation, using 'I' and being committed to your words.

3 Suggest solutions.

4 Conclude: finish off the interview. Draw up an action plan and schedule when necessary.

Table 8.5 Giving first-person feedback

'When you . . . '	Beginning with 'when you . . . ' describes the behaviour in a non-judgemental way, without interference
'I feel . . . '	Sharing the way in which the behaviour affects you, the impression it gives you
'Because . . . '	Say why you were affected in this way. Describe the link between the behaviour and your feelings
Break	Give the other person time to respond
'I would like . . . '	Describe the change you would like the other person to consider
'. . . because . . . '	It is a way of reducing the seriousness of the problem and being open to practical, constructive solutions
'What do you think?'	Listen to the other person's reply. Be ready to discuss various options

brilliant tip

The art of feedback

Whether you are mentor or mentee in the programme and thinking about your experience as manager, which boxes would you be able to tick today? Reflect on your daily conversations with your peers, colleagues and teams.

☐ Emphasise and reinforce positive behaviour

☐ Give descriptive, non-moralising feedback. Describe the behaviour and the effect it has on you. Do not try to evaluate or imagine the reason for the behaviour.

☐ Give specific feedback on particular points. General comments attenuate the effectiveness of the feedback and reduce its positive and constructive impact.

☐ Give feedback at the right moment. Give it immediately after observing an event that requires refocusing, unless emotions are running too high and it is impossible to handle at this moment. Choose a place and time when you can be quiet.

☐ As manager, during the annual review, prepare your message and the elements of language.

☐ Take responsibility for the feedback you give. You commit to your words. Use 'I' and not 'we', let others speak for themselves.

☐ Concentrate on the behaviour, subjects and practices concerned, and not the person themselves. Do not involve third parties.

☐ Eye-contact is essential. Talk to the person to whom you are giving feedback and look at them.

☐ Avoid abrupt shortcuts, brusque statements or categorical labels. Try not to generalise, don't use 'always' and avoid accusing words. Be specific and precise.

▶

☐ Concentrate on behaviour that can be modified. Give feedback on an element that the person can control and on which they have the means and the resources necessary to act.

☐ Do not overwhelm the person with more than they can take at once. Do not accumulate feedback.

☐ Do not mix positive and corrective feedback. Avoid 'it's fine, but . . . ' Even if corrective feedback finishes on a positive note, congratulatory, grateful or positive messages about specific actions do not mix with corrective feedback. Try to sequence your message, separating the two types of feedback. It is true that it is important to end corrective feedback on positive aspects. This relates to motivation and engagement by the colleague. A person will not modify their behaviour, way of working or communicating if they do not see the benefits to themselves. This is a golden rule for leading change.

☐ The recipient of feedback can compare your feedback with that of others, to see if they have noted the same behaviour.

☐ Qualities of feedback: immediate, descriptive, specific, acceptable, pertinent, concrete, verifiable.

During your mentoring conversation, feedback is more descriptive than evaluating. Mentor, your feedback is not a judgement. It is more specific than general. Mentees will also give you their feedback. It is reciprocal, taking account of the needs of the two of you. Otherwise, it could be destructive if the needs of the other person were not heard. Mentor, your feedback must be useful and directed towards behaviour so that your mentee can do something with it. It is suggested, not imposed. It is given at the right moment. It is formulated so that the other person understands it. Your mentee can reformulate it, in order to check they have properly understood it. Feedback allows the other person to know what impression they give, and helps develop and change their view of the world.

In the mentoring relationship, feedback is hugely important. Even if there is no hierarchical relationship between mentor and mentee, feedback follows the same methodology and requires the same care and attention as any other managerial conversation.

Mentors: Give an objective description of the behaviour, attitudes observed or evoked during discussions with your mentee. Recontextualise: analyse the impact this behaviour and these attitudes may have on your mentee's 'stakeholders' (line management, colleagues, customers, suppliers) depending on the situation. Move forward: make suggestions, encourage your mentee to consider what has to be done to change or adjust behaviour in a positive way. If you have a logbook of your discussions, explore with your mentee the facts and comments you have noted. Set them out and ask questions. Make sure you have understood: do not hesitate to ask for more information about anything that is not clear to you. Ask your mentee, when describing a situation, to recount their own words and gestures and those of the interlocutors. Ask your mentee what they think. Encourage clear thinking about yourself and then share your own opinion and analysis. Encourage self-analysis, independence and acceptance of responsibility about yourself and the effects of your actions and behaviour on others in everyday life at work. Round off the discussion, and ask your mentee what they think:

- What do you think about the situation you are describing?
- Do you have a view about what the others have said to you?
- What would you have liked to say in this context?
- I have experienced a similar situation to yours. This is what I said and did. What do you think about it?

At this stage you can adopt the particular approach of David Cooperrider and the Appreciative Inquiry model (Figure 8.5) to help the other person review a particular situation and put him or herself into it.

Mentors, using the above methodology, ask your mentees to describe the situation and its context: the specific discussions (written and spoken) and the people involved. Explore all possible scenarios with him or her. Ask them to imagine what the optimal situation might be. Invite them to design the specific stages to achieve the desired scenario: classify the situation according to a type. They could give it a 'title'. Ask them: what type of 'scene' do these facts represent for you? Why do this? When you name and describe a situation, you take ownership of it, which helps you to understand and assimilate it. You can add other elements in order to transform it in a positive way.

Mentors, ask your mentees to look at what they plan to do next with the various types you have identified together in their particular context. With your mentees, use the forward-looking dimension of change applied to the dynamic of self-knowledge.

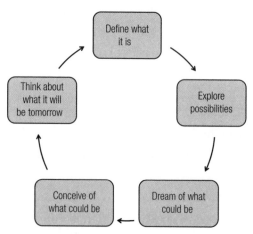

Figure 8.5 Appreciative Inquiry according to the David Cooperrider approach

brilliant exercise

Ask your mentee to do the following exercise. Accompany him or her in the process.

● Choose a situation from your present professional setting that you find difficult, and where you would like to see changes.

_____

_____

_____

_____

● Give it a title, and explain why you chose this title.

_____

_____

_____

_____

● Describe the possible scenario for change, using Cooperrider's model for inspiration.

　1　How could I analyse and understand the situation if I were not the protagonist in it?

_____

_____

_____

_____

　2　I describe several possible scenarios: how could the situation work differently, and for what reasons?

_____

_____

_____

_____

▶

3 I choose the best possible scenario.

_____

_____

_____

_____

How could I implement this in practical terms? I describe the resources, the means and the actions possible. I describe what the exercise has taught me, and how I can use it to help me move forward and visualise new and positive situations linked to the objectives I want to achieve or changes I would like to make, either in my professional circle, with its help if possible, or in my own practices.

_____

_____

_____

_____

I produce a list of 'scenes' on which I would like to work, giving them each a title:

title of the scene:_____

title of the scene:_____

title of the scene: _____

This exercise will help self-knowledge, a vital lever for success.

Work on the change. Change is both sequential and continuous, relying on constant self-knowledge incorporated over time.

List of open questions you can ask your mentee to enhance your feedback

Mentors, in the course of your feedback, and in order to pursue discussions with your mentee in more detail, the following methodology may be useful, with its 40 questions. A lot of questions, but read them all and try some of them. Don't forget to read them regularly! You can also use them in your day-to-day practice.

'Know thyself, and thou wilt know the universe and the Gods.'

Socrates

Think about this quotation from Socrates. Good self-knowledge maintains the consistency and stability needed in the identity ecosystem formed by our various ecologies (professional and personal). Self-knowledge also gives a better understanding of the landscape where you are developing. You focus on where you are today. You perceive who you are in this setting, and then you decode how you are perceived by your environment. You summarise what that teaches you, what that says about you and what it says about the landscape. You take a step back, an overview so that you can classify, prioritise and sequence your projects.

1   I think that what could help you is . . .

2   What worked for me is . . .

3   In my experience which was . . .

4   What you say makes me think that . . .

5   My reaction to your situation is . . .

6   If I understand you correctly . . .

7   I am curious to know if . . .

8   I wonder if . . .

9   Have you thought of . . . ?

10 What you say encourages me to think that . . .

11 What does that mean/mean to you/what else does it mean to you?

12 What importance do you attach to this belief?

13 What is your frame of reference for this?

14 What other context could you apply?

15 What do you think of that?

16 When you realise that, what does it make you think/feel?

17 And now you know, what do you want to do?

18 And what if you let yourself think, react differently?

19 What do you appreciate about this? About yourself in this experience?

20 How important is this to you?

21 How is this important/valuable to you?

22 What decisions motivate this?

23 So what do you want to do?

24 What would you like to do?

25 What do you tell yourself when you choose or decide?

26 Why is this important to you?

27 How would you like this to end?

28 What are you expecting?

29 What makes you think that? Feel that? Live in that way? Act like that?

30 Who says that you should do that? What rule governs that?

31 What would be a consequence of that?

32 What are you going to win or lose by that?

33 And what is that going to do to . . . ?

34 What does this word/term mean to you?

35 How do you define that?

36 What is the principle that guides you in this experience?

37 What would happen if you did/said, etc. . . . ?

38 What would you do if you knew what to do? Imagine you know what to do/say, what would you do/say?

39 What makes you say that . . . ?

40 What prevents/would prevent you from . . . ?

Points to watch

Mentors, during your feedback, don't forget your list of Dos and Don'ts.

Do:

- Listen actively. Teach by example. Encourage your mentee to move out of his/her comfort zone. Encourage independence, balance. Be enthusiastic in success, and show your pleasure.
- Encourage reciprocity. Be yourself and respect the mentee. Ask for help if necessary Ask non-judgemental questions. Know how to say: I don't know.

Do not:

- Fix the problem on your own, without the constructive cooperation of your discussions with your mentee. Angle for compliments and take control. Threaten or influence ill-advisedly. Let criticism show, without giving back anything positive or allowing a constructive scenario to be developed. Let the friendship dimension of the mentoring relationship obscure judgement and the authenticity of your feedback. Condemn and think that you are perfect. Take decisions for your mentee. Judge, evaluate your mentee. Give advice without explanation. Take a refusal to accept advice as a personal affront. Complain about your mentee in front of other people. Change your mentee or force him or her to follow your ideas. Project your vision of the world onto your mentee. Consider your own frame of reference exclusively.

Mentors, continue to provide regular feedback throughout the mentoring programme to maintain the effectiveness of your discussions with your mentees. This will also optimise preparation of your meetings.

Mentees, freely express your ideas and feelings and share your opinion with your mentor. Improve in the art of giving a response: clarify your requests, any disagreement on a situation or objectives or a plan of action, and say why. Formalise your thoughts in a welcoming, non-hierarchical environment, that will help you improve your feedback within your own professional setting. Learn to practise assertive behaviour with your mentor.

brilliant tip

Develop your assertiveness with the feedback from your mentor

What is assertiveness? Assertiveness[17] is a behaviour, a relational mode, supported by communication techniques (Figure 8.6). Assertiveness describes a way of communicating linked to both tolerance towards others, personal sincerity and a way of clarifying the message you want to express. When we are faced with difficult relationships and emotional situations, we tend to set up behavioural defences such as flight, aggression or manipulation. These behaviours are sources of tension, misunderstanding, loss of time and energy, and they drive us away from the core message we want to deliver.

Using assertiveness enables you to reveal yourself and to others. You will be respected and gain respect. You will develop good, interior confidence and identify your usual attitudes. You will know how to deal with passive, aggressive and manipulative behaviour and how to communicate effectively. You will strengthen your ability to set objectives, your analytical capabilities and ability to be objective. You will also strengthen your subjectivity by welcoming and identifying your professional and personal emotions. You will reinforce your capacity to forge an opinion for yourself. As a result, you will significantly improve your personal commitment in speech: the consistency between what you say and the way you carry your messages in voice and body language.

ASSERTIVE GOALS: POSITIVE CIRCLE

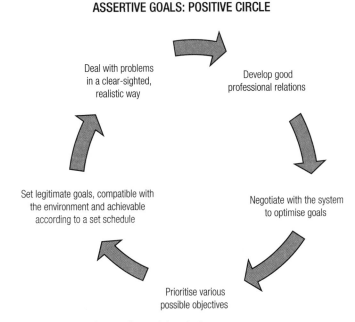

Figure 8.6 Assertive goals: positive circle

In a professional setting, with continuous just-in-time communications together with the demand for real-time responses, you communicate from morning till night; you exchange information, opinions and practise content curation – this task that has invaded your daily life, involving benchmarking and sharing content considered relevant. When you need to take a stand, there are possible conflict situations in the various interpersonal encounters concerned where you are exposed by your words especially if what is at stake in your communications may involve taking risks. If you want to place yourself at the right distance in the relationship to help create and maintain a channel of communication, so you see each other as mutually valid interlocutors, you have to express what you are – your emotions, what you want – your desires, and what you do not want – your limits. Faced with a difficult interpersonal communication situation in which you find it hard to express your point of view, your thoughts and/or a request, there are some techniques you can use.

The best-known assertive techniques are:

- *The broken record:* Repeat the same thing to express your point of view, like a broken record, until your interlocutor lets go. Repeating your first response as often as necessary helps to reduce pressure. So it is important not to respond to the other person's arguments, and not to counter-attack when presenting your own arguments.

- *The buffer technique:* You use the passive distancing illusion, to defuse any possible conflict. This technique involves responding using the reproaches you receive as the model, providing the buffer with the 'aggressor'. So if your interlocutor's statements involved known facts, your only response will be 'precisely', or 'that's true'. You allow the evidence, but not the consequences your interlocutor draws from them. This 'buffer' is especially effective in the face of ill-intentioned and badly argued criticism. If your interlocutor's statements involve criticism, an opinion or a value judgement, your response will be 'perhaps', 'that's possible', without engaging or entering into dispute.

Between mentor and mentee you will not necessarily have to use these techniques because your relationship is one of mutual goodwill. As a mentee, it will be very useful if you can discuss with your mentor in feedback that they might give you about your experience of using these techniques, and what you have learned in order to improve your everyday communications. Sometimes you have to give tough and difficult messages, without losing yourself or suffering negative effects for your self-esteem and confidence. Benefit from the experience of your mentor. Do not miss this opportunity! As you know now, mastering the art of communication will allow you to boost your career and to develop professionally in a very positive and powerful way.

● *The language compass:* The language compass will help
   you locate yourself in your communication and in the
   feedback dynamic (Figure 8.7). This is used to identify the
   language forms used, to ask the right questions to obtain
   the information you need. You need to locate yourself
   in the forest of communication. When speaking, try to
   identify what kind of verbal communication your speaker
   is using. This helps you understand what is important to
   the speaker and makes them aware of the type of verbal
   communication they are using. It helps you to ask the right
   questions to get to the point of your discussion.

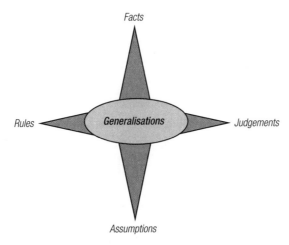

Figure 8.7 The language compass

Examples and questions for getting the right information in each of the following situations

Assumptions

> You say: '*He is not answering my emails. He must be unhappy
> with my work. I know what he is going to say to me.*'

> Questions to be asked: How do you know? What are you
> basing this on. . . ? How do you know that? What are you

basing it on . . . ? What does the fact of . . . prove that . . . ? What is the link you're making between X and Y?

You say: '*I am sure we will meet the target.*'

Questions to be asked: how do you know that . . . ? What are you basing it on . . . ? What proof/evidence do you have?

Rules

You say: '*It has to be challenged. Don't take risks. I can't let myself ask him that. It's not possible to do this. We must, we mustn't, we are obliged to, it's necessary . . . We must respect our line managers.*'

Questions to be asked: what would happen if we were to do it . . . ? What would happen if . . . ? What prevents you from doing it? What prevents me from doing it?

Self-imposed rules

You say: '*Don't take unnecessary risks. I can't allow myself to ask him . . . It is not possible to do it.*'

Questions to be asked: what happens if we take risks? What prevents us from taking risks? What obstacles would you face? What will happen if you . . . ?

Judgements

You say: '*One can't trust him.*'

Questions to be asked: how do I know? What creates trust?

You say: '*This person is not frank.*'

Questions to be asked: what makes me say that? What is a frank person?

You say: '*We can't trust him . . . People in this company are not involved. This person is not honest.*'

Questions to be asked: on what do you base your judgment? Do you have any proof?

You say: *'I am, he is, it's good, it's bad . . . '*

Questions to be asked: how is it . . . ? Who is it for . . . ? What makes you say that . . . ? On what are you basing your statement?

One fact

You say: *'It is important to maintain a good relationship. People must understand the project.'*

Questions to be asked: Ask using the 5Ws: Who, What, Where, When, Why? To make the facts clear, ask how something will be carried out/done.

You say: *'I would like my team to understand and take initiatives.'*

Questions to be asked: how will you know they have understood? What kind of initiatives?

Generalisations

You say: *'We can't change people. Always, never, nowhere, every time, everywhere, no-one, people, one. . . No-one ever listens to me.'*

Questions to be asked: Always? Never? All? Who is it? What people? Ask for a counter-example or an exception. Repeat the generalisation as a question. Offer a counter-example.

You say: *'They aren't going to be interested in that.'*

Questions to be asked: what is your basis for saying that?

You say: *'I do not like to upset people.'*

Questions to be asked: how do you know that you are going to upset them?

You say: *'Changing means losing my identity.'*

Questions to be asked: ask for an example. Does it mean you have never changed anything in your life? What have you changed already without losing your identity? What does it mean to lose your identity?

You say: '*I don't know how to express my opinion to a person in authority.*'

Questions to be asked: how does the fact that it is a person in authority prevent me from giving my opinion? What do I believe will happen if I do so?

You say: '*When someone controls me, I lose my own resources.*'

Questions to be asked: what precisely makes you lose your resources? What is the specific, direct relationship between control and your loss of resources? What does it mean for you to be controlled? Ask for specifics. Ask for exceptions. Reformulate the generalisation in question form and propose an alternative point of view.

Feedback in the mentoring relationship, just as in the professional relationship outside mentoring, is essential for better self-understanding and self-improvement. You will also better understand how other people operate. Reading and decoding your professional environment will become easier too.

Mentors, the quality of the feedback given to your mentees and vice versa maintain the quality of your mentoring relationship and ensure effective achievement of your respective objectives. High quality feedback enables both mentors and mentees to move forward on their career path and then transfer what they have learned and experienced within the dynamic of the mentoring relationship to their own fields and into their everyday working life. Giving quality feedback helps improve mentors and mentees' analytical and listening skills, and master the art of communication, a skill which serves the other skills.

The most efficient people are those who know themselves well and are able to understand others. The more someone understands themselves, the more they are capable of understanding others (Figure 8.8). The better they will successfully adapt to the constraints and requirements of the professional environment and the better they will communicate!

Learning how to give high quality feedback and consequently how to master the art of communication are two key factors that contribute to the success of a mentoring programme. Feedback and communication are on-going learning processes. Whether you are mentor or mentee, by improving and testing them within the safe, relaxing and hierarchy-free context of mentoring you will have a better chance of achieving your professional objectives once the mentoring programme is over.

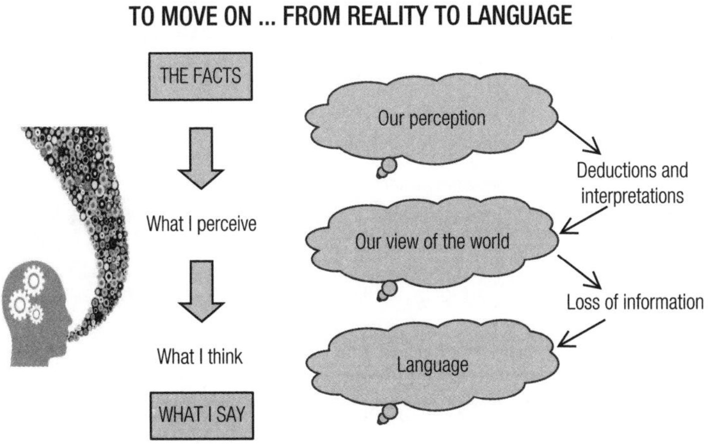

TO MOVE ON ... FROM REALITY TO LANGUAGE

THE FACTS

What I perceive

What I think

WHAT I SAY

Our perception

Our view of the world

Language

Deductions and interpretations

Loss of information

Figure 8.8 Who I am and where I am

 **recap**

In this chapter, these are the main points you need to apply when you give feedback in your mentoring conversations:

1　The quality of the feedback given between mentors and mentees is a key success factor in achieving your mentoring objectives and becoming a successful mentor or a successful mentee.

2　Qualitative mentoring feedback follows the same methodology as qualitative managerial feedback. Never forget that there is no hierarchical relationship between mentor and mentee.

3　High quality feedback goes with excellent communications. The more you master the art of communication, the more effective mentor and manager you are – improving your impact and bringing more consistency to your messages.

4　Don't forget this famous quote from Watzlawick: you cannot not communicate. It means that you cannot not give feedback!

5　Qualitative feedback is a question of communication, mindset and posture.

6　Mentees: give your feedback to your mentor freely. Improve the art and practice of giving a response, clarifying your points of view and your demands – and the art of questioning.

Mentors:

1　State the constructive nature of your feedback: your feedback is more descriptive and inspiring than evaluating.

2　Take responsibility for your feedback: use the first person singular.

3　Check understanding when giving your feedback.

4　Help your mentee improve their way of doing feedback. Teach them techniques like DESC or assertive communication.

5　Facilitate self-lucidity and self-responsibility.

6 You can use techniques like Appreciative Inquiry from Cooperrider and use the art of writing possible scenarios for leading change; use the assertiveness techniques and the language compass.

Ending the programme

The mentoring programme has to be completed properly and the conclusion of the mentoring relationship and of the mentoring process as a whole evaluated. During the programme, the various staging points within both mentor and mentee communities have helped to support participants, share experiences and complete regular evaluations.

At the end of the mentoring journey, active participation by mentor and mentee and their mutual commitment will be evaluated. Mentors and mentees, what was the level of your involvement in and commitment to the programme? How did you keep to your schedule? Have you always been available for appointments and meetings? How did you manage imponderables?

The evaluation will apply to the mentoring relationship and to the quality of the relationship: the level of satisfaction and sense of comfort within the exchanges. Mentors and mentees, how will you evaluate the level of effectiveness regarding the dynamic and the content of your exchanges? How do you rate the level of satisfaction with your exchanges? The quality of communication will be evaluated too. Mentors and mentees, how did you show active listening? How did you master the art of questioning and improve understanding of the content of your exchanges? Regarding the ethical framework, mentors and mentees, did you respect confidentiality? Did you show goodwill and authenticity? Did you comply with your role as mentor or mentee? As for the objectives set at the beginning of the programme, have you been able to complete them? Did you establish and follow up your action plan? Did you develop professionally and personally?

In your final mentoring conversation, mentors and mentees, ask yourselves the following questions, before you produce your own final report:

- What have we accomplished?
- Have we succeeded in what we set out to do?
- What have we learned during the mentoring process?
- What type of learning have we done?
- How can we use this knowledge?
- Have we achieved all the objectives?
- What skills has the mentee been able to acquire?
- What are the benefits the mentor was able to analyse?
- Shall we continue this relationship informally?
- Are there actions to carry out after the mentoring programme?

brilliant exercise

1 As mentor, how have I incorporated the various staging points to adjust my objectives:

_____

_____

_____

_____

2 During the mentoring process, have I identified development?:

- In my relationship with my mentee:

_____

_____

_____

_____

● In my attitude as mentor (listening, communication, feedback):

_____

_____

_____

_____

● In my personal objectives:

_____

_____

_____

_____

3 Am I able to evaluate the impact of my experience as mentor on the
   following?:

   ● My professional environment:

_____

_____

_____

_____

   ● My professional practices: (management, planning, strategy,
     decision-making, risk-taking, etc.):

_____

_____

_____

_____

   ● My career development (transitions, opportunities, promotions, etc.):

_____

_____

_____

_____

▶

 ● My know-how-to-be (executive presence, leadership, communication, etc.):

_____

_____

_____

_____

4   Do I want to continue to be a mentor within my organisation?

   ☐ Yes:

_____

_____

_____

_____

   ☐ No:

_____

_____

_____

_____

   ☐ And/or be involved in internal leadership of a mentor community:

_____

_____

_____

_____

Mentors may decide to continue the mentor experience outside the organisation by forming links to associations, business start-ups, ex-employee groups, students or young professionals. In this way, they can commit to share their expertise in different environments.

▶ brilliant exercise

1 As mentee, how have I incorporated the various staging points made
   during the mentoring programme to clarify my objectives and realise
   them through effective action plans?

   _____

   _____

   _____

2 During the mentoring process, was I able to identify developments in my
   relationship with my mentor?

   _____

   _____

   _____

3 Am I able to evaluate the impact of my experience as mentee on the
   following?:

   ● My initial expectations as I entered the mentoring programme:

   _____

   _____

   _____

   ● My professional practices: (communication, management,
      leadership, risk-taking, etc.):

   _____

   _____

   _____

   ● My career development (transitions, opportunities, changing job,
      etc.):

   _____

   _____

   _____   ▷

● My know-how-to-be and my personal development (confidence, self-affirmation, visibility, leadership, etc.):

_____

_____

_____

4   Do I want to become a mentor within my organisation or outside my organisation?

☐ Yes:

_____

_____

_____

☐ No:

_____

_____

_____

☐ And/or be involved in leadership of an in-house community of mentees:

_____

_____

_____

Feedback from the mentoring programme takes the form of a meeting attended by all the participants, based on a number of evaluations made during the course of the programme. The steering committee may then decide to continue the mentoring programme according to the objectives it sets and based on the pilot programme put in place. Mentors and mentees may wish to continue the support as informal exchanges, a positive move that emphasises the effectiveness and success of the programme. It is still important to offer the mentoring experience to other participants and to give mentors the option of capitalising on their experience and continuing it, if this is the aim of the organisation.

During the mentoring programme, mediation is offered to deal with any problems the mentors and mentees may find and wish to express outside of the staging points. This is done by the external expert adviser who has a neutral position with regard to the organisation. The content of the mediation will naturally remain confidential. Individual support is therefore proposed outside the staging points made during the programme, to meet the individual needs of mentors and mentees as closely as possible within the situations they find. The external adviser provides a kind of hotline for the mentor and mentee, if needed, having the skills and expertise to deliver this support.

During the mentoring programme evaluation process, any occasion when the need arose for mediation will be reported. How many times was it needed and in what specific situations? The external adviser may be assisted by expert facilitators trained in mentoring, who will collaborate in this process.

Testimony from mentors at the end of the programme

Key concepts

Here are some testimonies from mentors who have been engaged in individual mentoring programmes.

Very enriching experience. It is interesting to work with my mentee on his career development, awareness of his own values and all that over the long term. It's worthwhile to see the mentee's objectives gradually realised.

Positive impressions in both directions! A success!

Openness, transparency and sharing experience! Unexpected as far as I'm concerned.

Interesting to discover the vision of the youngest people in our Group.

Figure 8.9 Key words from mentors' testimony

As mentor, one has much to give them. But after a few sessions, it's easy to run out of steam without preparation.

Very enriching experience, helped me to develop my listening and empathy skills, to take a step back and analyse, to pass on what works, the right attitude, sufficient knowing how to be.

It is important to know how to listen and it's good practice for active listening without being inhibited by management or judgement of others.

It helped me to know the Group and its organisation better, as well as the strengths and weaknesses of other entities.

It's given me an idea! Apply to myself what I pass on to him!

Informal relationship, without management, and therefore simple. Open, direct contacts. Objectives given, followed and achieved. Flexibility in the diary which helps meetings.

Transparency: be able to tell each other everything! Dialogue. An easy relationship. Talk about myself and my career path in an entirely different way.

Relationship based on trust between two people. We are each listening to the other.

An enriching, sympathetic experience that helps in taking an objective view.

Good experience and relationship for both of us. This has helped me to be aware of my positive impact in terms of having confidence in someone else.

The mirror effect, awareness of my own practices and enrichment of my professional experience, by this experience and these discussions: the feelings of my mentee have cast a different light for me on subjects such as management, leadership and risk-taking. I am careful to apply the observations gained during this exercise to interactions with my own teams and my manager.

Enhancing my ability as a coach, to share my own experience and professional life. Satisfaction in giving concrete and useful help. I hope I have improved my listening skills.

Supporting generation Y. Along with my mentee I have found other ways of looking at work and the company.

Reminds me how far collaboration is a lever of choice for performance! Be exemplary!

Everything I have learned will not just be useful for myself alone.

Be challenged in ways I never expected to happen again. Break through the routine 'bubble' a bit like taking time out even if you don't have any, where there is space to share about essential things like career, practices, the company, etc.

Become a model within the company. Valuing this experience within the company. In the end, I am a leader.

It's restored my confidence in business.

Testimony from mentees at the end of the programme

Key concepts

Here are some testimonies from mentees who have been engaged in individual mentoring programmes.

I have really valued the quality of the relationship with my mentor, a relationship truly based on trust, listening and sharing. In a major Group like ours, the fact of being 'mentored' by someone from one's own organisation is valuable. It gives unparalleled freedom of speech.

The mentoring relationship is a career 'booster' that helps one travel a long way along the personal and professional path very quickly.

I hugely appreciate the experienced, neutral and positive insights of my mentor, who can help me take a step back from my own situation, as well as drawing positive lessons from it, and gives me very pragmatic advice (professional situation, attitude, etc.).

Figure 8.10 Key words from mentees' testimonies

An enriching experience, that makes me want to be a mentor!

Importantly, the programme (documentation, practical sheets and initial meeting) as well as the relationship with my mentor have helped me define my career path clearly: short-term, medium-term and long-term employment objectives.

Mentoring has helped me understand how to succeed, inspiring me with the experience of another professional who has succeeded in turn! Doing this from what I am, from my own organisation's processes and culture. My exchanges with my mentor have been effective and constructive. In one word, true! What I didn't really expect, even though we were told this at the start of the programme. This gave us both room to manoeuvre, a freedom for analysis and the option of thinking about scenarios that were not in my initial scoop!

Friendly, stimulating and confidential listening.

I shared my perceptions of my environment without any managerial constraints. After a short learning curve at the start of the relationship, I felt really free to express my problems, without mixing it up with a friendly relationship.

My mentor gave me some very sound courses of action, as well as theoretical contributions to my objectives.

My mentor helped me develop a network. He opened up my internal network, and also gave me specific ideas for developing an external network, which had not been my priority.

Preparing for interviews allowed me to ask myself questions that I had avoided, and let me lean into the future.

I have learned a lot from the work of defining and clarifying what I was doing, before meeting my mentor. This helped me in my reflections and helped me frame and nourish our discussions.

I gained a broader knowledge of other jobs and areas of business in my Group, as well as career opportunities, and I was able to put my own position into perspective.

This programme exceeded my expectations! I gained a much better understanding of professional relationships towards management and my peers.

It is a very well-structured support process!

It's not easy to talk about oneself, one's ambitions and doubts, but the effort my mentor demanded of me helped to make it really positive. Preparing for the interviews I asked myself questions that I would certainly have avoided before, I now try to look objectively at myself and to lean into the future.

I am very glad to have had the opportunity to talk about my work and my career, outside a hierarchical context, without evaluation, with someone friendly who was extremely open to listening.

It is an enriching programme for the mentee, and I am sure it is for the mentor as well. It helped us face up to ourselves, to ask the right questions and take a step back on what we are and what we want to do. And for both of us to grow.

This experience has helped me to build my medium-term objectives and to break them down into short-term objectives, to work at on a daily basis. It has also made me aware of the difficulty, but nonetheless of the necessity of setting time aside for reflection.

Mentoring is a brilliant and special way of spending time with experienced managers and leaders from my organisation, who have generously given their time to contribute advice and feedback.

I had difficulty expressing my ambitions and my doubts. The mentoring relationship is a powerful and positive channel for expressing personal things that one would not say elsewhere, and that have a direct impact on professional life every day and in building one's career.

A discussion with someone able to understand my problems, but who nonetheless is outside of my own field of work. An advisory approach, dedicated to making progress!

A great adventure, in both human and professional terms! I would really have liked to have had one day's immersion in my mentor's professional life!

It greatly helped me to look ahead, to prepare the next step, and not look just through the prism of my present position.

The end of a mentoring programme is vital, because this is where the whole programme is evaluated, the dynamics involved, for both the mentors and mentees and the company, the progress made and benefits obtained by mentors and mentees. It is also a time for sharing among mentors, mentees and the members of the steering committee, the chance for the organisation to value the commitment of mentors and mentees. A good analysis at this stage allows the company and the organisation to update and profit from the thorough development achieved by mentoring on both professional and personal developments. This explains its attraction, its necessity and success, since mentoring is a unique way of combining human development with performance.

Mentoring programmes allow your companies to detect problems in the field that have not been noticed before, such as knowledge of jobs and responsibilities, lack of overall communications, a clear view of leadership and management practices. The mentoring programme report encourages subsequent action to help employees as well as the organisation itself to make progress. It is the power of mentoring to initiate and mobilise energy and talent for leading necessary change in the longer term.

 **recap**

In this chapter, these are the main points you need to recall when it is time to end the mentoring programme:

1 Synthesise the different staging points organised during the whole programme. At each staging point, mentors and mentees will debrief and answer key questions.

2 Evaluate mentor and mentee commitment to the programme.

3 Evaluate the quality of the mentoring relationship: the mentor and mentee's level of satisfaction with their exchanges, and the quality of communication – feedback, listening and understanding.

4 Evaluate the way mentors and mentees have complied with their respective role.

5 Evaluate the way mentors and mentees have kept to their schedule and managed imponderables.

6 Evaluate the way mentors' and mentees' objectives have been completed and how relevant the exchanges have been.

7 Evaluate the impact of the mentoring experience on mentors' and mentees' professional environment, practices and career development.

8 Before the closing meeting, mentors and mentees are invited to make their own evaluation and to share their evaluations with each other.

9 Organise a closing meeting with all the participants and the steering committee. Facilitate sharing among mentors, mentees and the members of the steering committee.

10 Value mentors' and mentees' commitment.

Notes

1 Peter Sloterdijk, translated from *Eurotaoismus: Zur Kritik der politischen Kinetik* (1989).
2 Ibid, p. 100.
3 Ibid, p. 102.
4 See Chapter 4, the list of possible individual mentoring objectives on p. 44.
5 Hagakure, *The Book of the Samurai*, ed. Yamamoto Tsunetomo, trans. William Scott Wilson (Kondansha International Ltd., 1979).
6 To some extent this is your personal risk-taking, revealing and sharing truthfully your individual perception of your career path. So it is important and vital to agree from the outset on the ethical charter for confidentiality and mutual commitments. An interview between the participants, both mentors and mentees, is useful at the start of the programme to confirm these aspects, over and above the documents to be signed and the unsolicited applications to join mentoring programmes, which are more and more popular nowadays.
7 The same procedure applies as for the preliminary interview with mentors and mentees, to confirm their applications to the programme, or to make managers aware of the process.
8 Hannah Arendt, *The Human Condition* (Chicago: University of Chicago Press, 2nd revised edition, 1999).
9 Do you incline towards the famous, three-bladed instrument of torture, the 'trepalium', the etymological root of the French word 'travail', 'labour', or rather do you prefer the word 'opera', the Latin root of the French 'œuvre', 'artistic work', opening up for you the potential for self-realisation?
10 Axel Honneth, *The Struggle for Recognition: The Moral Grammar of Social Conflicts* (Cambridge: Polity Press, 1995).
11 François Dupuy, translated from *Lost in Management* (Paris: Seuil, 2011).
12 Michela Marzano, translated from *Extension du domaine de la manipulation: De l'entreprise à la vie privée* (2010).
13 Comes from the nominative, neuter past participle of the Latin *obicere*, 'place before'.

14 All forms of cultural, political or religious extremism, all forms of racism, sexism and discrimination arise in fact from the false belief that one's own frame of reference is the only true, valid point of view, and thus must be imposed on others.

15 Alfred Korzybski, philosopher and scientist, was the founder of the subject of general semantics.

16 This method of questioning was developed two centuries before Christ by the Greek rhetorician Hermagoras, then taken up by the Roman teacher Quintilian, who set out a logical schema for questioning to optimise analysis of the situations encountered, collecting the information and all the data around a particular issue.

17 Chambers Dictionary and the OED mention the common noun: 'assertion': a positive statement or declaration, as well as the adverb 'assertively': with the character of assertion. The verb, 'assert' means: to affirm, defend one's rights in the context of the non-violence movement begun by Gandhi and Martin Luther King. Assertiveness was also examined by the psychologist Andrew Salter during the 1970s, and later by the psychiatrist Joseph Wolpe who defined it as: *'any expression entirely free of emotion towards a third party, except for anxiety'.*

PART 3

Be a successful mentor and manager

CHAPTER 9

Being both a
mentor and a
manager: how
to switch from
one to the
other

How this chapter will help you

Understanding what management and mentoring refer to is key to your development as a manager-mentor. The more you learn to improve your skills as mentor, the more efficient you will become as manager. Then you perfect your leadership. This chapter will help you to be both a manager and a mentor to become an even better leader.

Clarity of mission and vision for the organisation is an important function of management and leadership. This chapter will help you understand how to analyse your industry or sector, and identify the drivers for change in your environment.

As we saw in Chapter 6, there are four possible attitudes the mentor can take, depending on the mentee's profile, including that of the manager-mentor. This necessary adjustment implies the use of situation-based mentoring. How is it possible to be manager and mentor at the same time? When and how should you move from one role to the other? First of all, let us look at the roles and expectations of the manager.

What is management?

Management exists to keep organisations on time and on budget. Management refers to the technical procedures to organise and to administer an entity or a business unit. It is generally understood that management comprises several components. Managing is about dealing with and creating effective relationships with employees, hierarchy, clients, suppliers and investors. It is about finding and giving information, including high quality feedback, regulating communication flow and organising logistics. Management can be divided into two parts: (1) operational management; and (2) people and relationship management.

Managers' main responsibilities

Regarding operational management, as manager, you will have to set targets or goals. You will organise planning and task forces. You will establish detailed steps to achieve your targets, including timetables and guidelines. You will develop specific skills to manage in 'project mode': from matrix management to cross-cultural management. You will allocate resources and budgets to accomplish plans. You will do your best to solve problems, to monitor and evaluate results – identifying deviations that are usually called 'problems'. In other words, operational management is about coping with complexity and processes.

Regarding people and relationship management, you will be asked to set objectives and performance standards based on the position, the results and the actions – not on the individual. Measuring performance using Key Performance Indicators (KPIs), career planning, structuring and staffing jobs, providing development and training courses and monitoring key behavioural competences will fall within the scope of your work as manager. In this way, management coordinates teams and helps personal development.

What does a manager do?

As manager and decision-maker, your aim is to ensure organisations function properly in terms of operations, finance, lead-times, etc. coordinating people and teams and evaluating performance. You motivate people and bring them together as regards evaluating performance and achieving quantified and qualified objectives. You have organisational authority. You handle inter-personal relations to achieve specific, organisation-related objectives, without necessarily 'inspiring' future co-leaders, as the leader may do, although managers and business leaders each construct strategies of alliance and influence. As manager, you mainly put your colleagues, peers and teams forward for superior positions and jobs in order to respond to organisational objectives defined by management strategy. Your manager's authority is built into the formal position held in the organisations.

Ideas associated with the concept of manager are shown in Figure 9.1. Managers and mentors help support, develop and manage people.

Figure 9.1 Management key words

What does a mentor do?

Whatever the mentor's level, position or experience, the role is built on the following 10 key skills:

1 Self-awareness.

2 Commitment to own learning.

3   Interest in helping others develop.

4   Behavioural awareness (others).

5   Listening and communicating.

6   Managing relationships.

7   Goal clarity.

8   Analysing and conceptualising.

9   Business and professional savvy.

10 Focus on building on strengths and minimising weaknesses.

When managers use the skills of mentors and act as mentors themselves, they create a better professional environment to nurture the development of skills and they manage their teams better.

Let us look at six managerial situations:

1   Monitor daily tasks.

2   Delegate.

3   Evaluate.

4   Showcase colleagues.

5   Develop a strategic vision of your position within the company.

6   Anchor your working base in values and a philosophy of work.

1 Monitor daily tasks

Managers tell you what to do and when to do it, without necessarily sharing your sense and overall vision of your routine and of the tasks required: reporting, deadlines, meetings, revisions, project management, etc.

Manager-mentors share the 'why' and the 'how'. Through modelling and reflecting on their roles, they encourage sharing of ideas and thoughts in their interaction with colleagues, over and above the tasks that have to be performed, at a meta-level that promotes managerial skills and initiative.

Managers, when you give out tasks to be performed, share your vision of 'why'. Sharing the vision of things does not mean breaking the necessary lines of management, nor the organisation of the work itself. On the contrary, it enables better understanding of what has to be done, forms the bond with your colleagues and encourages commitment and effectiveness. Commit to the process of professional development with your colleagues in the longer term, despite tight deadlines and daily pressures. By developing this attitude, you encourage managerial skills, mentoring and independence among your colleagues and teams, that will save time for everyone and improve interpersonal relationships. Better interpersonal communications create a better working environment. Share your vision!

brilliant exercise

- How do you go about sharing work out among your various colleagues?

  _____

  _____

  _____

- What type of communications do you use?

  _____

  _____

  _____

- How are your orders perceived?

  _____

  _____

  _____   ▶

- Do you think you are a manager-mentor in this context?

  If yes, for what reasons? Describe the elements that come into play here, in a factual way.

  _____

  _____

  _____

- If not, what are you missing? What do you need?

  _____

  _____

  _____

2 Delegate

Managers delegate and divide up the work to optimise efficiency. Managers allocate and assign work, sharing out tasks according to skills and positions, they control, but they should never get involved in terms of sharing, exchanges, or even solutions found, because of their own workload and schedule.

Manager-mentors collaborate and help to find resources. Mentors practise the art of listening and get involved, no matter what their position in the hierarchy. They activate specific mentoring skills, such as interest in other people's development, the capacity to analyse human behaviour and soft skills, to share, guide and collaborate. Managers, when you delegate in order to share the workload, develop mentoring skills. Get involved at a higher level with your colleagues and your teams: help in the completion of tasks to be fulfilled, access to resources and information *to make a better contribution to results, even indirectly.*

brilliant exercise

- Are you available for your colleagues?

  _____

  _____

  _____

- What type of professional relationship do you have with your colleagues and your teams? How would you classify your professional relationships?

  _____

  _____

  _____

- What level of commitment do you have with your colleagues?

  _____

  _____

  _____

- Do you facilitate the work of your colleagues in terms of networks, resources and sharing of information?

  _____

  _____

  _____

3 Evaluate

Managers evaluate performance according to objectives that they allocate to their collaborators, assessing missions carried out and completed, and their organisation's own assessment processes. They must comply with internal procedures.

Manager-mentors advise and give guidance on knowing-how-to-be and on career management, above and beyond the processes to be followed to achieve objectives and develop within the organisation.

Managers, in annual appraisal meetings and your daily conversations, advise and guide beyond the processes. Manage every day by increasing your colleagues' empowerment. Welcome and accept constructive comments. Give qualitative feedback by structuring your communication in three stages:

1   Begin with something positive.
2   Say what you think, to help your colleagues or teams to develop and to improve the tasks that you give them over the allotted time.
3   End with something positive.

Think about holding congratulatory meetings: take the initiative for the meeting! Go straight to the point. Highlight success. Do not hesitate to show that success does not happen on its own, and that problems have been overcome. Express your feelings, for example, 'I was delighted by your success!' Let the colleague say what they have done: ask questions, ask for details. Make yourself available, give your time. Ask the colleague if this success could be applied in other situations, if the team could benefit from it, and if so, how. Finish on a positive note, without going on to another subject.

---

brilliant exercise

● What does performance mean to you?

_____

_____

_____

● What does it mean for you to evaluate your colleagues? How is this useful?

_____

_____

_____

- Do you assess your colleagues every day?

_____

_____

_____

- How do you use the evaluation processes in your annual interviews?

_____

_____

_____

- Is evaluation synonymous with professional support for your colleagues?
  - If it is, explain how these two notions are combined in your practice, and what you do to act in this way.

  _____

  _____

  _____

  - If you do not think these two notions are combined, explain why, and what you do to support your colleagues and teams.

  _____

  _____

  _____

4 Showcase colleagues

Managers often fail to promote their colleagues, on the basis of personal agendas and internal competition. This explains why, in order to progress, employees normally change company. It is sometimes the only way of breaking through the glass ceiling because it is impossible to get your own performance valued. Affirming and praising others, in this negative logic, means exposing your own weaknesses or revealing your own personal agenda.

Manager-mentors do value people. They minimise weaknesses and highlight the talents and skills of their colleagues and their teams. In this way, they help them value in turn the people with whom they work.

Managers, consider valuing your colleagues and cultivating quality relationships. Proper, honest evaluation of work done and the quality of managerial relationships are levers to nurture motivation in colleagues and help them become good managers who will know how to cultivate their own mentoring skills. So a 'good manager' has a role that includes both transmission and exemplarity. They know how to gather a circle of competent people who will become vectors for passing on leadership of the manager-mentor who in turn will be able to value and support them.

⤴ brilliant impact

'Fish for the relationship' or how Bateson showed the importance of positive feedback to maintain the quality of relationships in a learning context.

The biologist, anthropologist and philosopher, Gregory Bateson studied dolphins in the Virgin Islands in 1963, then later, along with a pair of ethologists, he continued the study at the Sea Life Park in Hawaii until 1973. In their research programme, these ethologists used huge pools in which the dolphins were exposed to conditioning experiments. Their trainers threw them fish to reward them. Each animal therefore learned to link the reward to the correct response. There then came a phase in which the trainer no longer rewarded a repeat behaviour. The dolphin showed its impatience with a noisy beating of its tail after several fruitless attempts. This 'gesture' was then rewarded: the trainer gave it 'unmerited' fish, to maintain the relationship within this context of learning and evaluation of a behaviour performance. These fish acted as positive feedback without being linked to an actual reward.

One day, on returning to the experiment pool, a female went through a whole string of behaviours, four of which had never been observed in this species before. Bateson recorded this scene and studied it. It seemed to show that the animal was attempting to invite further 'unmerited' fish rewards, as reciprocal positive feedback gestures, thus maintaining and preserving the relationship between herself and the monitor. The experiment had helped to trigger innovation within this learning context. Bateson used these observations when he was further exploring the relationship we human beings have to our work, and how we learn to learn.

The parable of the dolphin emphasises the learning/evaluation-valuation/recompense dynamic. Of course, we are not dolphins! Nevertheless, in our professional relations and working life today, with the overwhelming number of things to be learned and done all day, every day, it is important to be aware of how difficult it is to learn how to learn – the action-learning principle – which is part of the process for successful performance. It is also important to understand the various kinds of feedback that are effective in validating and encouraging learning, nurturing our motivation in order to maintain interpersonal relations and create innovation.

People must be self-motivated to achieve a high level of learning. Just like the dolphin, an employee who tries to learn how to be more effective must initiate changes in their own behaviour, depending on context, and react to the different kinds of feedback received. A manager-mentor will understand how to protect and nourish the relationship, in order to help in the most difficult and demanding kinds of learning.

brilliant exercise

● In your everyday managerial conversations, do you practise valuing people?

_____

_____

_____ ▶

- Do you value the successes of your colleagues?

  _____

  _____

  _____

- Are you aware of the way your colleagues learn to learn?

  _____

  _____

  _____

- Do you give time to your colleagues for advice and guidance about their professional practices?

  _____

  _____

  _____

- What specifically does the term empowerment mean to you with regard to your relationships with your colleagues?

  _____

  _____

  _____

- Like the parable of the dolphin, how do you maintain the quality of the relationship with your colleagues?

  _____

  _____

  _____

5 Developing a strategic vision of your position within the company

Managers are aware of the need to develop a strategic vision of their position within the company. This vision influences the relevance and validity of their own objectives and the objectives they themselves will define for their colleagues in the medium and long-term. The context of an organisation is always fluid, and change is now a permanent feature of the business world today.

The manager-mentor will advise their colleagues, depending on the company's strategic development. They will share the necessary information they need in order to adjust their attitudes and the content of their positions. For instance, the manager-mentor may advise a colleague to spend more time on strategy than on purely operational matters, in order to follow the strategic line and capitalise on the potential of their position, while also adapting to the needs and vision of the company. The manager-mentor will help the colleague to optimise their position in the company, provide guidance to become more visible, select the best projects and contribute to create a reputation linked to a strategic legitimacy.

brilliant exercise

- How do you help your colleagues to develop a strategic vision of their position?

  _____

  _____

  _____

- Do you advise your colleagues so that they can bring their position alive and embody their own functions in the best way?

  _____

  _____

  _____

- Do you advise your colleagues so that they can develop and move on to a better position? Do you set objectives to advance this process?

  _____

  _____

  _____

6 Anchor your working base in values and a philosophy of work

Managers work in a quantified, measurable way to achieve the organisation's objectives. They themselves are obliged to report to their line manager, which means they have less room for manoeuvre, and the pressure applied to their colleagues increases.

Manager-mentors have person-centred values that affirm and create meaning, going beyond measurements, figures and processes. This aspect makes the setting and conditions for work more pleasant, and reduces pressure associated with the workload. Sharing values helps retain talented people more effectively. Over and above the pressure of numbers, the manager-mentor develops a mind-set that enables them to stand back and get things in proportion. And never to forget the values that give meaning and carry the vision necessary to bring people together and move forward as a group.

brilliant exercise

● Describe your ideal manager-mentor:

_____

_____

_____

_____

_____

● Where do you stand in relation to this picture?

_____

_____

_____

_____

_____

As manager-mentor, you also need to be supported so you are not alone in confronting your challenges. Think about creating a community of manager-mentors to share best practices and encourage a culture of cooperation. Don't forget that mentoring is an excellent way to do it!

brilliant recap

In this chapter, these are the main things you have to keep in mind when you want to excel at being both a manager and a leader:

1 Management exists to keep organisations on time and on budget.

2 Management divides into operational management and people and relationship management.

3 To be a great manager-mentor, integrate the major 10 mentor skills in your management practices.

4 Think about your managerial situations and conversations. Work on how you can integrate successful mentor postures and attitudes in your communication and behaviour.

5 By using mentor skills and acting as mentor, you will create a better professional environment. You will inspire co-leaders and optimise your alliances strategy and you will improve your decision-making process. You will then become a better leader.

CHAPTER 10

Use mentoring to increase commitment and motivation in your team

How this chapter will help you

Mentoring is a powerful tool for developing what we have called 'collective intelligence', meaning 'making people work better together and use their talents and their energy in the best way!' – we could even talk about 'empowerment through mentoring'. This chapter will help you to increase commitment and motivation in your team.

Mentoring enhances your individual capacity to express your skills, potential, ideas and your professional emotions in a workplace environment that accepts and integrates them, while regulating their expression. This enables you to transform your individual potential into collective resources. Gathered in this way, these resources add a further dimension in terms of human capital and professional value.

 'When you ask people what they understand by "belonging to a super-team", the most frequent response is how meaningful the experience is for them. They talk about being part of something bigger than themselves, being connected and creative. It seems clear that for many people, their experience as members of a great team forms a very intense part of their life. Some spend the rest of their life trying to rediscover this environment.'

Peter Senge[1]

The mentoring process uses integration as a tool for encouraging the development of a 'learning organisation', to use Peter Senge's term. In this environment, learning to learn becomes possible, easy and attractive within a global vision and a culture of empowerment. The mentoring culture specifically encourages the use of behavioural and relational talent as a resource with which to work on building a 'learning' collective. Mentoring provides a way of reflecting on your own mental models, on all of your conceptions (limiting and/or enriching), on obstacles, on possible inhibitions: those associated with the organisation and those related to your own professional and personal development. The mentoring culture applied within an organisation provides the opportunity to be both learner and trainer in turn. Be ready to learn and become a super trainer!

Mentoring is a successful process because it can fit into the logic of your company's performance and strategy objectives. Professional mentoring actually offers an effective strategy for making the most of people with potential, helping the positive growth of leadership models at work within the company. By linking younger, talented people and those with potential together with experienced leaders and top performers, the group of mentees targeted by the mentoring programme will learn faster and rapidly take up positions with a greater degree of leadership involved. This creates positive outcomes for both your company and for the individuals themselves.

Mentoring strengthens commitment to your own job while also giving leverage in terms of quality and transformation for the organisation's performance and its internal resources. Mentoring develops loyalty, shapes high performers and those with potential, increasing their commitment by bringing them into contact with a broader spectrum of the organisation's business and operation. Mentoring thus gives them the opportunity to learn what they need to perform well in their jobs while opening up new horizons for leadership and promotion.

Mentoring creates a rich learning environment, effectively using and developing the organisation's human resources to make progress and contribute new energy and vision. Mentors and mentees, you become ever more closely involved and responsible within your organisation. With greater commitment comes increased motivation (Figure 10.1). And when motivation increases, commitment grows. This is a virtuous circle, a positive dynamic.

Mentoring helps employees to gain knowledge, skills and expertise to nurture their own professional development and employability, as well as helping the organisation remain competitive as it continues to invest in its employees. Mentoring is a very effective approach to using, developing, distributing and transforming ability and knowledge into values.

Mentoring is a very concrete way to apply individual and collective empowerment. It is a vector for change, situation-based and transformative, that combines organisational, business and strategic needs with personal needs to influence the creation of a new collective. By sharing and discussing in mentoring

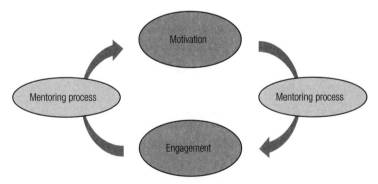

Figure 10.1 Mentoring and motivation

conversations, in either individual or collective mentoring, you create a positive culture, new reference points and markers, a different history and a common language for your organisation. This enables you to settle and to find your place while also having sufficient room to grow.

Mentoring enables overall mobilisation of all forms of knowledge within a professional identity: knowing, know-how, know-how-to-be, know-how-to-become, and the fifth knowledge: know-how-to-be-visible through digital identity. Motivation is built when there is a balance between the skills you mobilise – your qualities and talents – and the business context of your company or organisation.

Of course, people who are working are motivated by what they earn, but not only by that. The sense of forming part of an organisation with a specific objective, and contributing to this goal, is very important. This feeling nurtures your sense of self-legitimacy.

As manager-mentor, it is important to understand how these three systems overlap:

1 the personal system of self-empowerment;
2 the organisation's system of empowerment;
3 the motivation system.

1 The personal system of self-empowerment

People nowadays have a greater involvement in and responsibility for their own professional life. This involvement is built on self-knowledge, self-enterprise and self-management. You as an individual are treated as a strategic entrepreneur of your own life, and within this context, you practise continuing self-management. You are faced with the need to apply self-empowerment.

Within the global market, personal empowerment is both a requirement for the external market, and a means to manage competition effectively within the organisation. To remain employable, you have to locate where your professional identity lies at all times. You are asked to manage your portfolio of activities and your image. To achieve these objectives you are asked to do many different things. You seek to optimise the quality and impact of your interpersonal communications constantly, and deepen your knowledge of your working environment. You have to extend control over your environment and knowledge of the ground. You need to develop a strong political sense and to be comfortable with social interactions. You take calculated risks, and deal with stress while trying to grow professionally and settle into a positive dynamic.

You need to deal with all these parameters, which can adversely affect your motivation as an employee, facing new styles of management. The mentoring relationship acts as a compass to guide you, helping you to prioritise imperatives and also discuss solutions for the best possible response, leading to the most suitable and the most realistic attitude.

The better people can manage these imperatives, the better they know themselves. The better they know themselves, the more capable are they of developing strategies for dealing with environmental demands (Figure 10.2). Self-empowerment strategies contribute to a continuous, self-management process:

Self-management leads to a pragmatic methodology. Your employability is linked to the ability to mobilise yourself, to align the power to act within an empowerment process. The greatest challenges are to express objectives clearly, to stay comfortable within the professional environment, and to

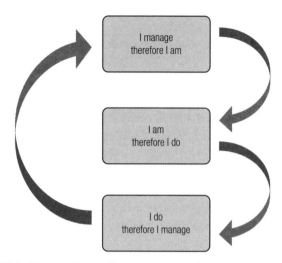

Figure 10.2 Manager's paradigm or strategy of empowerment

maintain the available energy capital to deal with problems in the business and in the world of work.

Maintaining a high level of motivation comes from a methodology based on thorough self-knowledge and continual analysis of environmental data. This is an aspect that mentoring can assist with, leading to concrete results over the long term.

Managing your own professional life in this way involves looking for tips and tricks to bring good news to the table, being seen as a positive influence, a mascot for success against the competition, keeping up an attractive level of employability both within and outside your organisation. It means that you and the people you work with can capitalise on your own advantages, to be ever more competent, pro-active, visible, better, etc.

Pressure on you to deliver on all fronts grows exponentially – while you must also remain free and 'happy' to be assessed continually. It is a kind of paradoxical dictate on working people, explained by the fact that employees' competence in their job is subject to the imperative to deliver results, and is no longer considered simply the means to do the job.

In this context, you and your colleagues have to create the conditions for your own empowerment. How will you succeed? By showing external evidence of mastery of the workplace. Your subjective interiority is put on stand-by, for the sake of an apparent external control. You will continuously seek to eliminate internal constraints. You will practise intensive personal development, in order to increase self-knowledge, self-management and self-improvement. At the same time, you will continuously seek to eliminate external constraints. You work to improve your organisation, in order to obtain the conditions for your own empowerment within your job, ensuring good employability, both in your company and on the job market.

As manager-mentor you need to understand better how motivation works, and how it is linked to this way of managing professional life to help employees practise self-empowerment, so they have to ask themselves the following questions:

- Can personal development be identified with the performance of organisations?
- Does what businesses want match what employees want?[2]
- Are companies' objectives the objectives of employees?
- What is the share of personal responsibility in professional management of success and failure?
- Can you truly create the conditions for your professional success?

These questions will allow managers-mentors to be more effective in their work and better identify the factors that motivate those they manage.

 **example**

Individual empowerment may be described as a continuous control loop built around five imperatives:

1 Having a personal debrief: mapping yourself.

2 Listening to others and their feedback.

3 Confirming any reality gaps: integrating your whole circle.

4 Managing professional aspirations linked to your personal development.

5 Developing the ability to mobilise and motivate.

Understand that you have to practise every day to perfect your routine and to get new positive habits. Don't get discouraged! We spend our time learning and forgetting things we should do. Be patient with yourself and take time to integrate and to apply this methodology.

2 Empowerment by organisations

Empowerment of individuals is a strategy needed by organisations and companies to move forward, be competitive and also stay 'human'. Empowerment is a broader process for involvement and positive promotion of individuals, to improve the way they live together and feel satisfied at work, thus benefiting the performance and durability of the business.

Practising empowerment is a way of working actively on lack of motivation, or lack of a shared vision, on objectives that are less encouraging, or disconnected from the ground.

These gaps between employees and their businesses interfere with the overall system, and have a negative impact on the organisation: significant staff turnover, lack of engagement among colleagues, communication problems, damage to financial performance, frequent reorganisation injurious to management, poor management structure, etc. Setting up an empowerment culture involves organisations in the implementation of a strategy for collective intelligence.

Collective empowerment encourages individual power and potential, effectively mobilising the capacity to act, thus releasing creative energy. It helps to grow an economy of human values, creating space between a company's or organisation's economic objectives and professional and personal development.

As a tool for applying empowerment, mentoring promotes employee autonomy and helps them to develop as creators of meaning and quality value. The mentoring process helps to set up a dynamic and motivating ecology between individuals and their environment (technical, managerial, business, social). Collective 'intelligence' and empowerment are thus the result of the mentoring that produces it.

For your organisation, the implementation of empowerment is measured by the actual results produced by your organisation: flexibility and sharing of information, horizontal communications, reducing costs and overspend, better financial performance and effective ethics.

Personal empowerment practised within your company is measured by your employees evaluating execution of a task against four criteria:[3]

1 *impact*: personal conviction that the task to be performed will produce a desired effect;

2 *competence*: personal conviction that they are able to successfully perform a task;

3 *meaning*: personal conviction that a task will meet your aspirations;

4 *choice*: personal conviction that actions are self-determined.

If these are strong convictions, your employees will undertake the tasks with greater motivation. This evaluation gives them a perception of the way their abilities and tasks are valued within the environment.

For your company, benefits of empowerment strategy include: closer involvement and increased commitment of your employees, greater motivation, creation of a setting to encourage innovation and increase competitiveness and productivity, more appropriate risk-taking and clearer decision-making and a better quality of customer service.

3 The motivation system

Employee satisfaction leads to commitment – a real performance booster. Having committed and loyal employees is a measure of success for an organisation. Payment is often considered a motivating factor. Position in the company, social prestige associated with a position, projects led, the internal culture, the market sector, teams, opportunities for development, for travel: these are also motivational. Everyone has their own motivation, and each one is valid.

Mentoring helps to evaluate motivation, identify reasons why it might be missing and correct this by working on the factors the mentoring programme has brought to light. By facilitating open discussion and interaction, without a hierarchical overlay, mentoring is a valuable tool for the manager since it gives access to employees' professional as well as social and psychological needs, all of which play a part in motivation itself.

For instance, what gaps and links are there between KPIs and the single question: what is important for you?

 **exercise**

The following questionnaire will help you examine the level of your current motivation. You can also use these questions in your managerial conversations, to probe the motivation of your colleagues. These are also questions that may be used in mentoring discussions, to explore the mentee's professional situation.

Questions about my own motivation:

1   What interests me in my work?

   _____

2   What am I passionate about in my work?

   _____

3   Does my work match my aspirations?

   _____

4   Does my work help me to discover the challenges that motivate me?

   _____

5   Can I take initiatives?

   _____

6   How do I contribute to achieving objectives set by my managers?

   _____

7   Does my work contribute to the work of other employees?

   _____

8   Does my job have meaning?

   _____

9   Who am I helping?

   _____

10 Do I have enough help in my work?

   _____

11 Do I notice signs of recognition in my circle?

   _____

12 Do I accept feedback from others?

   _____

13 Do I ask for feedback?

   _____

14 Do I give sincere feedback to my employees, my peers, my teams, my management?

   _____   ▶

15 Within my professional environment, am I able to express my ideas and communicate them clearly to others?

_____

16 What signs of acknowledgement do I give to others?

_____

17 What are my criteria for experiencing recognition?

_____

18 What are my criteria for feeling satisfaction and motivation in my job?

_____

19 Are my criteria external, controlled by others, or are they internal and under my control?

_____

20 Do I feel part of a group? A working community? A company?

_____

21 Do I feel I exercise a positive influence on my working environment?

_____

In order to maintain motivation in your teams and employees, as manager-mentor, you have to try to create a collaborative environment, accept and consider more flexible practices and working methods, and be ready to integrate changes. Knowing how much managing a hierarchy is vital, you will do your best to master the art of delegation, allowing your colleagues to take the lead in some tasks. You will set up an open culture in which the other managers are approachable and accessible, encouraging an authentic, consistent managerial culture and regular communications. You will allow feedback from others about yourself, about the organisation and the way the business operates. You will try to offer places for socialising not directly linked to the business, in order to create links and meaning other than in terms of performance.

Both individual and collective mentoring create communities that act directly on motivation. Forming non-hierarchical, collaborative communities meets the social need for belonging that links all the people within an organisation. The conditions for doing your job, and the need to practise self-empowerment for the sake of professional development make such supportive, facilitating and effective communities very important, since they are directed at solution-sharing. Within this positive 'ecology' created by mentoring, mentors and mentees can freely discuss the way to deal with organisational problems – governance, objectives, strategy, vision – as well as problems associated with the job they do – working methods, management, leadership or career progression.

Training colleagues in mentoring, in order to create a pool of mentors, is a positive way for the manager-mentor to support the company in the process of change, and to give colleagues and peers the option of joining a process of empowerment.

Becoming a mentor is a major step in the empowerment of organisations. It means adopting a practical work philosophy that contributes what is missing, beyond the financial aspects associated simply with pay.

brilliant recap

In this chapter, these are the main things you have to keep in mind to increase commitment and motivation in your team through mentoring:

1 Mentoring enhances individual capacity to express skills, potential, ideas and professional emotions.

2 Mentoring is a very effective strategy for making the most of people with potential.

3 Mentoring helps the positive growth of leadership models at work within your company.

4 Mentoring creates a positive dynamic. Mentoring strengthens commitment, offers a rich learning environment and attractive learning organisations.

5 Mentoring helps employees to gain knowledge, skills and expertise.

6 Mentoring boosts professional development and employability.

7 Mentoring is a very concrete way to apply individual and collective empowerment as mentoring empowers both people and organisations. Collective empowerment encourages individual power and potential, mobilising the capacity to act.

8 Mentoring maintains a high level of motivation based on thorough self-knowledge and continual analysis of environmental data.

9 Practising empowerment is a way of working actively on lack of motivation.

10 Individual and collective mentoring both work on the ecology of performance in a new, innovative and attractive way.

Notes

[1] Peter Senge, *The Fifth Discipline: The Art and Practice of the Learning Organization* (New York: Random House Business, 2nd rev. edn, 2006).

[2] This is the issue explored by Italian philosopher Michela Marzano, translated from *Extension du domaine de la manipulation: De l'entreprise à la vie privée* (Paris: Fayard/Pluriel, 2010). She writes that there is no link between the capacity for self-determination (choosing one's own conception of life) and the choices an employee has to make in business.

[3] Kenneth W. Thomas and Betty A. Velthouse, 'Cognitive elements of empowerment: an "interpretive" model of intrinsic task motivation', *The Academy of Management Review,* October 1, 15(4) (1990): 666–81.

CHAPTER 11

Improving your own leadership and interactive skills through mentoring

How this chapter will help you

In order to improve your own leadership skills, it is essential to know what leadership is and what kind of skills have to be mobilised if you are to succeed as manager and mentor. This chapter will help you understand how to use skills gained through individual and collective mentoring to reinforce your leadership and to perfect your communication. You can then discover if you have these skills, how to acquire them if you do not and how mentoring can help you with this!

As we have already noted, there has been a great deal written about leadership. Leadership is the key concept for business, and a real headache for managers, and no doubt for you as well! Despite everything said on the subject, it does not mean we know any more about it, or that we are clear what leadership models are important and necessary. Do you know what the leadership models are in your company?

Let us address this question. Leadership is a complex notion, at the intersection of management, experience, a particular understanding of situations – in the field – and an individual's ability to influence and build a team around them. In other words, your leadership is a wise mix of your managerial practice, your experience, your ability to analyse your professional environment and your own personality. Your personality is formed of the traits in your own character which help you to be influential: your behaviour and the way in which you communicate. Your ability to form alliances and weave a firm network also forms part of the leader's 'toolkit'.

Leadership is an interactive process, at the heart of an influence web, within the feedback loop between leaders and followers. The leader ideally has a dual role. They encourage sustainability and stability of the organisation, by embodying its culture and dynamic energy. What is meant by the organisation's dynamic energy? It is the ability of a business to get moving, to develop and implement appropriate strategies to reach its goals. The leader may be said to start the organisation moving. They know how to change the rules when necessary. The leader can start the company moving because they also have their own dynamic. The leader enables change to happen through the future-oriented vision that they carry and embody. It may seem a little complicated, but this means two things. The leader supports what is working well in the organisation, everything that makes it endure and remain steady. At the same time through the vision and movement embodied in the leader, they help the business to progress and develop. Stability and movement are thus the two defining characteristics of leadership. These two concepts may sometimes seem mutually incompatible.

Over and above their role as manager, the leader infuses meaning into individual and collective performance. That is why expectations today are very high around leadership perceived as an open system. There are a number of questions to ask about leaders: what kind of leaders do organisations and businesses need? What style of leadership should be preferred: inclusive? participatory? inspiring? visionary? communicative? transformational? The challenge is to identify the type of leadership, in terms of governance and practice, that will allow businesses, including yours, to optimise the way they work and to use the resources and talents of each person in order to establish a true strategy of empowerment.

How are leadership and mentoring linked?

Mentoring enables leaders, managers and teams to work specifically on existing models of leadership in your businesses, and on new models of leadership to be created. Mentoring helps what might be called an open leadership process. Leadership is considered an open, interactive system, allowing collective reflection on the subject in hand.

What then becomes of the idea of authority, linked to individual decision-making? Considering leadership as an open system does not mean eliminating any kind of order and hierarchy that maintain the coherence of a business and an organisation. Nor does it eliminate individual decision-making, especially the particular moments when, after discussion, consensus or negotiation, a leader has to decide alone.

It is interesting simply to see the positive effects of mentoring in a business, when the mentoring culture is implemented through mentor and mentee communities that share and exchange information, breaking down barriers to communications, changing mind-sets and 'silo thinking' habits. How does a hierarchical organisation integrate and cohabit with the barrier-free communities created by mentoring? How do mentoring communities affect notions of hierarchy and change management practices: organisation management and people management? What type and concept of leadership produce these mentoring communities? This is where the question of the relationship between authority and leadership lies.

What is the difference between leadership and authority?

Formal authority describes a legitimate power relying on the status of a person, enabling them to carry out activities and influence other people's behaviour. Personal authority refers to an informal aspect of power associated with character traits, the ability to impose yourself. Leadership can also rest on a statutory power: a hierarchical position defining rights and responsibilities, duties and privileges of the people who enjoy it. Leadership is thus associated with an individual's ability to influence and to attract others according to the position held within an organisation. It does not mean that the leadership that relies on a statutory power is authoritarian – although there may be a great temptation on the part of the person in that position to impose their authority.

Leadership also relates to an intrinsic personal power: a personal capacity to influence which is exercised independent of any official position. What is influence? An active process that enables guiding, modifying decisions, thoughts, beliefs or behaviour of a person or groups in terms of actions and responses. Leadership is the exercise of influence that encourages willing attraction to an individual by people or groups, by virtue of that individual's personal characteristics and/or position. That is why leadership forms part of a shared construction within an open and interactive system.

What is a leader?

The leader is someone who bonds people, groups and organisations, using an interactive dynamic to achieve specific objectives. The leader is typified by their ability to mobilise and bring others on board to achieve actions aimed towards a specific goal.

A leader does not necessarily hold a formal position. The leader often exercises 'flexible' or 'soft power' to implement strategies of influence. The leader has skills in collaboration and communication, and encourages support. The leader knows how to develop leadership characteristics in others and create strategic alliances. The leader motivates and brings people together around the vision they carry and embody. They inspire co-leaders who transmit and share the same vision. The leader develops independence, creativity and initiative in their colleagues. The leader knows how to step outside the ordinary to offer a new vision and openings to new prospects in terms of business, strategy, management of human and managerial resources.

The leader can demonstrate managerial courage, taking difficult decisions after learning through experience, sometimes in a costly way, to deal with the three categories of people identified by the famous Chinese philosopher Confucius: 'When you do something, know that you will have against you those who would like to do the same thing, those who want the opposite, and the vast majority who do not want to do anything!'

Facing the leader are internal/external competitors, those opposed to the leader's actions and those who do not want to participate in the leadership dynamic. In this context, the leader has learned to face the unexpected, to control negative forces and to integrate complexity. There are not in fact three but five categories of people whom the leader has to learn to face, in order to strengthen their leadership.

In businesses, as well as in any kind of organisation, when someone wants to lead a project, take decisions or move forward with processes, people and business, there are normally five types of people:

1 People who support a project, a vision, an idea or a change.
2 People who are open to a project, a vision, an idea or a change.
3 People who are cagey about a project, a vision, an idea or a change.
4 People who are strongly opposed to a project, a vision, an idea or a change.
5 People who are neutral about a project, a vision, an idea or a change.

Through experience and the 'striking force' or strength of their alliances (network and co-leaders), the leader identifies these categories or people and can create the optimal conditions to realise objectives, by using their professional experience to develop their leadership skills all the time.

The leader capitalises on and models a career-long professional path. The leader knows when and how to step back to see the big picture, and may depart from the solitary attitude intrinsic to the leadership position to rely on a network of allies, followers and co-leaders. And in relying specifically on this network they can better reintegrate and live with a form of solitude intrinsic to the leadership position, used in decision-making.

 **brilliant** tip

Some concepts associated with the leader

Guide; influence; gather together; inspire; bear a vision; interact; align around an objective; unite; drive; innovate; create; communicate; develop; take decisions; exemplarity; authenticity; integrity; forward-looking; charisma; strategy; persuasion; communication; trust; values; ethics; transmission; emotional intelligence; social and political skills.

The leader's power reflects a behaviour that expresses personality, qualities of analysis, relationships and a forward-looking way of thinking. Today's leadership styles are directed towards models that are collaborative and inclusive, looking at the long term, not just the short term. These are leadership models that can address the imperatives and challenges of the global market, the need to innovate in organisations to improve individual and collective performance.

Everything is asked of the leader today! As leader in your company, you have to take account of smooth, real-time communications, of total hyper-connectivity, of the demands of competitiveness and performance, managing and retaining talented people, change management, handling restructuring and continuous improvement processes in organisations, even though you have neither the time nor the resources to do all this. Not to mention people who want to move around or leave the organisation, all of which will necessarily affect your level and style of leadership!

As one of 'tomorrow's' leaders, you have to be able to create short-, medium- and long-term visions, provide sustained support through change while bringing people and groups together, and if necessary to modify governance, processes or ways of working. Because of that, and because you cannot do all that successfully on your own, leadership is no longer considered a single-handed, autocratic and solitary practice. Leadership has become an open system: dynamic, interactive, participatory, collaborative and inclusive. It promotes improvement of what your organisation already has, and is empowering in terms of capacity to act for individuals and collectives to find responses to challenges now and in future.

What type of influence do you have?

Here, in general terms in Table 11.1, are the differences between the influence exerted by a leader and that by a manager who also has influence in their position in the company.

Where do you recognise yourself here?

These two models of influence, *soft* and *hard*, are not mutually exclusive, but complement each other in the very exercise of power. The 'hard' aspect of power is associated with the formal, regulated power of influence exercised by the manager. In their practices, leaders and managers mobilise the components and qualities associated with either of these two types of influence. In this sense, managers and leaders as users and purveyors of sources of influence, have complementary roles.

Table 11.1   Types of influence

| | Types of influence | |
	Leader 'Soft power' influence	Manager 'Hard power' type
Behaviour	Attract, motivate, bond and include	Persuade and control by use and application of internal procedural rules
Resources	Communication Inspiring interaction	Evaluation and reward system
Main notions	Charisma Inclusive persuasion Setting the example by embodying and committing to the vision Emotional and situational intelligence: capitalising on existing resources and innovating Placing the structure within a dynamic and a movement	Processes of evaluation, compensation and promotion Setting the example by committing to appropriate internal procedures Organisational intelligence Maintaining consistency of structures over the long term

So people in managerial and influential positions have to develop the ability to use both the 'hard' and 'soft' aspects of power and switch between the characteristics of each of these, according to the demands and a clear-sighted analysis of the situation encountered. In other words, they have to become leader-managers or manager-leaders, depending on the position they occupy! And also be able to train their 'followers'! It is easier to support an authority when you are sharing in meaningful projects, ideas, strategies and work that can motivate and unite people.

Should we replace management with leadership? Management and leadership serve different functions. We need both management and leadership. When we do need more leadership, we paradoxically focus more on management. The result: we end up with over-managed and under-led organisations. The highest aim: trying to provide leadership when you are managing. Leadership means taking an organisation into the future, finding and exploiting opportunities quickly. Leadership is about vision, producing constructive change. Leadership is not about attributes, it is about behaviour. We need more people to be leaders, no matter where they are in the hierarchy.

Are you able to switch from one attitude to another, and gain agility in integrating these three dimensions and functions: manager, leader and mentor? Today is your big challenge! Your companies will be better balanced if they let their employees act in all three dimensions – manager/leader/mentor – and allow them to gain the skills they need, with the necessary training and strategic roles. As an open system, leadership particularly calls into question the dimension of 'support without challenging or putting hierarchical pressure onto colleagues', that is embodied in the figure of the mentor. By applying this attitude of leader-facilitator, the manager can become a mentor.

Leadership is aligning people with a vision and values. What key actions can be put in place to develop leadership skills to integrate the other two dimensions: operational management and mentoring of colleagues?

---

brilliant exercise

What kind of a leader are you? Take stock of your practices and ask yourself the right questions to review your skills as leader and the way you express them:

1 How good am I at taking decisions? How do I measure this?

2 How do I implement the decisions I take and get them applied?

3 How do I organise follow-up of decisions taken?

▶

4   Do I know how to choose and be decisive, depending on circumstances, for myself and for my professional circle?

5   How do I control the effectiveness of my action plans?

6   How do I maintain a heading?

7   How do I consider and accept my responsibilities?

8   How do I carry out a project or a vision?

9   Do I know how I pass on my ideas, how do I do this?

10 Do I know how to influence, and how do I do this?

11 How do I encourage support?

12 How do I unite and gather?

13 How do I communicate around myself (line managers, teams, colleagues)?

14 Am I willing to take risks?

15 How capable am I of wanting to do what I do not know how to do? How capable am I of learning and projecting myself?

16 Am I ready to accept difficulties, and how do I do this?

17 Am I able to bounce back? To transform a negative experience into a constructive step?

18 What is my strength?

19 What is my resistance potential?

20 Do I learn from my successes?

21 Do I learn from the problems I find?

22 How do I react to adversity?

23 How do I combine visibility, exposure and political games?

Take stock of your skills as leader in three stages:

1   First of all, choose the 10 questions of those above that immediately attract your attention. Work on them. Analyse what they mean to you in terms of your professional situations. The context of the situation, the people involved, your actions and reactions.

2 Once you have sufficiently considered these aspects of leadership in depth, in the light of your own experience, move on to further questions, working in the same way.

3 Produce a description of your leadership: strong points, variations and new insights.

Now you have produced your own portrait, let us go on together to consider some key leadership behaviours, and how mentoring can help you.

Focus on six key behaviours for leaders

1 Be inspiring. Develop a vision of the future! Create an inspiring vision and share your vision! Give direction and stretch goals

State your vision, based on a precise goal, suggest objectives and open up to the future. Question experience to explore other ideas and find different ways of acting and moving forward. Not to mention . . . ! Constant questioning of experience takes place in mentoring conversations. Questioning experience is the objective of mentoring. Include collective mentoring sessions that work on this subject, and ask your questions: how do I state a vision, how do I make it real? How do I communicate upwards? To whom, and in what order? Is this a vision that will carry people along with it? How can I confirm that it is good? What are the criteria for this? What type of influence do I need to use to offer it to others: soft or hard? What worked and what failed? And when it was difficult, or when there was a setback, what did that teach me? Share your case studies and your experience on this topic, in very specific terms, during the collective mentoring sessions. You can run collective mentoring sessions yourself on this subject and get help from an external expert activity facilitator. Joining an individual mentoring programme will also help you. Matching up with a mentor who has experience in this area will also help you address your ideas and methods on how to carry forward, affirm and achieve a vision for a situation, a project or a strategy.

2 Share values

Make sure that the values you promote are shared. Find out what values your peers, colleagues and teams carry and communicate themselves. Choose a mentoring position in your managerial conversations and in guiding your teams, during meetings, for instance. The framework of exchanges initiated by a mentoring approach in your role as manager-leader will allow your colleagues to express what is important for them: the values with which they are associated.

3 Lead by example. Practise what you preach

Consistency is a fundamental aspect of leadership. Showing consistency between what you say and what you do significantly increases your impact as leader, as well as the possibility of attracting co-leaders and followers. Consistency in the leader contributes to consistency in their messages, increasing the impact of what they have to say. Adopt a mentoring attitude when you speak and communicate. What does this mean? It means you are supporting and sharing, rather than assessing and exerting power. You are soft rather than hard. You are consistent and you know how to see the big picture, stepping back to consider both positive and negative features.

4 Lead change

Support for change, the ability to drive an organisation and its individual members mean the leader has to take risks and strategic and influential decisions. When you lead major change, using a mentoring attitude helps you facilitate integration of the change in the organisation. Take risks and create change. Share risks and hardship. Manage change strategically. Manage resistance to change by listening. Give your people time to assimilate and understand the benefits of change, new vision and strategy. Talk positively about change. Be adaptable and responsive to change.

Adopting a mentoring attitude will allow you to reassure others, since you are welcoming the feelings of your colleagues and teams about work, whatever they are. You are not judging them. This does not mean that you agree with everything you hear. Empathy is not sympathy. You are also able to demonstrate an executive and inspiring presence linked to the consistency of your attitude and of the messages you want to convey. You affirm your leadership by leading change like a mentor. The more you embody the mentoring attitude as manager, the more will you develop a leadership style that corresponds to what is expected of you: ensuring the durability of your company, while also contributing dynamism!

5 Build and lead a team

As a leader, use mentoring skills to build and to lead a team. How can you do it? Develop a human network to achieve your goals: create teams and networks that understand the vision and strategies and are committed to this strategy. Keep people moving in the right direction despite major political issues, bureaucracy and scarce resources. Communicate regularly. Try to implement an 'open' culture in which managers are approachable. A mentoring culture helps to establish this open culture. Facilitate cooperation by talking to your people and by listening to them, providing high quality, authentic and positive feedback. Involve everyone, trust your people and rely on their judgement. Bring out the best in your people. Create a group dynamic and help your team reach better decisions. Try to give your people varied work. Monitor progress in a positive way and facilitate team self-assessment. Lead as you would like to be led: do not over-boss. Cross boundaries to find new leadership models by helping your people to work together across natural barriers that occur inside and outside companies (hierarchy, functional silos, differences). Look for new ideas. Share with your peers and with people at different levels inside and outside your company. Benchmark the best practices in your company and outside it.

6 Communicate

Communicate the way mentors talk to their mentees in the mentoring conversations. Communicate guidance by words and deeds. Communicate in a clear, articulate and audible manner. Be an effective listener. Use appropriate questions to gather information.

Vary your communication style to suit your audience. Present information in a way that engages others. Use logical persuasion, outline pros and cons of different approaches to win support. Share knowledge and experience with others across your company. Seek to understand people's different views before influencing. Communicate with the right people in the right way.

Finally, develop a leader's mind-set, allowing you to use your mentoring skills to develop leadership skills and mobilise them in all managerial situations. Be open-minded and be willing to try new ideas and approaches. Generate ideas and fresh insights and seek better ways of doing things. Remain confident and positive in conditions of uncertainty. Show resilience, despite obstacles, disappointments or in the face of your challenges. Be flexible and open to understanding other people's perspectives. Find solutions to problems by collaborating and sharing knowledge and experience with others to improve performance as a mentor does. Question traditional approaches and challenge where appropriate. Be open to ideas. Empower, motivate and inspire people around you. Align, motivate and inspire people. Be enthusiastic and try to create a positive work environment. Delegate and encourage creativity in the people you lead. Demonstrate confidence with respect and trust without courting popularity. Communicate openly and honestly. Give clear guidelines and set clear expectations. Empathise and listen with understanding. Be willing to discuss and solve problems. Give support and help.

brilliant recap

In this chapter, these are the main things you need to keep in mind in order to become both a manager and a leader:

1 You must understand what leadership means, and what the expectations of leadership are within your company or organisation today.

2 Knowing how to switch from manager to mentor will increase your leadership skills. Start by analysing your leadership skills and the different contexts in which you show and express them.

3 Leadership is a mind-set that you will experience and understand better in a concrete way through individual and collective mentoring. Keep in mind that mentoring and leadership are both situational, and therefore linked to your experience and all the lessons you have learned. Mentoring will give you the opportunity to capitalise on all that you have learned up to now.

4 A mentoring culture within your company will help you to bring more leadership skills to your current managerial conversations and situations. Don't hesitate to join a mentoring programme or ask for it if there is not one yet.

The manager-mentor-leader is the new figure that meets and addresses the needs of most organisations today.

CHAPTER 12

Cross-mentoring and e-mentoring: exciting new ways of working

How this chapter will help you

Mentoring programmes adapt to companies' needs and challenges. This chapter will help you to understand all the combinations that mentoring programmes can offer.

The simplest and standard form of mentoring programme is in-house individual mentoring that brings a mentor and mentee together for a specific period, on average for one year. This programme takes place within an entity or business unit. When the programme involves different sites, entities or subsidiaries of the same company, it is called individual cross-mentoring. There are two types of individual cross-mentoring programme: individual cross-mentoring within a company; or mentoring across companies in several businesses within the same sector or in different sectors.

The individual cross-mentoring programme is generally focused on the same development objectives of individual and collective performance and managing talented people as for a more straightforward individual mentoring programme. The difference lies in the fact that the individual cross-mentoring programme has a broader pool of mentees and mentors. A group or organisation has to ask for mentors and mentees in several entities and geographical zones. Thus, individual cross-mentoring deploys a broader mentoring community within one organisation, or else creates a new external professional network, when individual cross-mentoring is organised within different companies. Cross-mentoring is a device that applies its method for empowering individuals to a broader population: it stresses construction, anchorage of forces and talents while trying to minimise potential problems.

The individual cross-mentoring programme therefore involves breaking down barriers, maximising transverse connections, so your company is choosing to link up people not normally in touch with each other, and who did not know each other previously. This is what traditional individual mentoring programmes do already. In an individual cross-mentoring programme, this aspect is deliberately strengthened. Your company can choose to set up an individual cross-mentoring programme between people in different subsidiaries. If these subsidiaries are in a geographical area accessible to participants, mentors and mentees can meet up face to face. If the subsidiaries are abroad, discussions can be by webcam, Skype, email and phone. So, for instance, the mentoring programme feedback may lead to a final session attended by all participants and organisers, where everyone has the opportunity to meet and share, if the budget allows. This final session could be combined with a global seminar, an annual event of the internal network, if the company holds one, or a congress, to keep the organisation's costs down.

Why do in-house cross-mentoring?

You can set up in-house cross-mentoring within your business, for instance, because you wish to change or improve business or managerial practice, improve communications or develop innovation. Such a programme will encourage the sharing of best practice, assisting the transmission of tips and advice, for instance, to improve internal communications within a major industrial or financial group. It is not always easy to understand and decode the communication method to be used within an inter-cultural/inter-entity transverse context. Individual cross-mentoring will counter withholding of information, in a positive way, by developing inter-entity cooperation practices and can improve the flow of internal, inter-entity information.

Cross-mentoring will also help you improve your inter-cultural management practices. Are you working with teams in different countries? Have you already had training in inter-cultural management that has given you a good grounding, but is not enough for you? Supplement it with in-house cross-mentoring. In this context, mentoring will help you directly address your perceptions about the problems you meet, and will find solutions for better shared working. You can then offer these solutions to everyone involved in this situation in your Group. The same goes for practices around business: strategy, customer relations, managing competition.

Cross-mentoring therefore helps you work on developing performance on a broader level, incorporating greater complexity and a wider range of differences between people and practices. It helps to raise awareness, unify and strengthen the internal culture of a Group or an organisation at a higher level. Cross-mentoring actually strengthens internal cohesion on a much broader scale, and is a vector for distributing the company's core values. Cross-mentoring creates wider communities, a new type of network that is a real resource both for your company and for you.

As with any mentoring programme, the population involved in the individual cross-mentoring programme has to be targeted, according to the objectives your business has set for itself. Does it involve enhancing the skills of a group of managers from several entities? Does it involve building up a group at a particularly challenging level of management, rethinking leadership models and managerial practices?

Or building an under-represented category, women, for instance, in responsible positions and at executive level?

Decide on the form of the programme! It is important and vital to assess the individual cross-mentoring programme. Why do you want to implement this programme? What are the initial needs identified? Who is the programme for? Identify the recipients of the programme. The population chosen to receive the programme will determine its type and design.

For instance, cross-mentoring can be set up in the form of reverse mentoring, to raise awareness in 'seniors' about the use of NICTs by giving them mentors from generation 'Y'. As for cross-cultural mentoring, this applies to groups who need to learn about cultural diversity.

Think about the methods of delivering the programme and ask yourself a number of questions. What is the framework for discussions between mentors and mentees? What type of ethical code applies to this context? Will there be two-way contracts between mentors and mentees, or else three-way mentor–mentee–company contracts? What form will the process of matching and the selection criteria for participants take? Will you set up a steering committee for the programme? If the individual cross-mentoring programme involves subsidiaries in different countries, what local intermediaries will you have?

Cross-mentoring also allows you to increase the number of mentors. The mentor–mentee pair may be extended with a third person to capitalise on the mentoring synergy and increase its effectiveness. A mentee may have two mentors in two subsidiaries, on two different sites. Individual cross-mentoring programmes thus boost individual performance and enable collective reflection on new ways of working and organising work.

Figures 12.1 and 12.2 show you the matrix of various possible combinations for mentoring: from the simplest to the most complicated.

	Mentee	Possible contacts for the mentee		
Collective cross-mentoring	1 M or 1 F	**Mentees** several M several F group	**and**	**Mentors** several M several F group
Collective mentoring	1 M or 1 F	**Mentees** several M several F group	**and**	**Mentors** several M several F group
Individual cross-mentoring	1 M or 1 F	**Mentor** 1 M/F _ _ _ _ _ _ _ *duo*	**and/or**	**Mentors** 1 M/F + 1 M/F 1 M/F + 1 M/F _ _ _ _ _ _ _ *trio*
Individual mentoring	1 M or 1 F	**Mentor** 1 M/F _ _ _ _ _ *duo*		

Maximising transversality and breaking down barriers

Developing collective intelligence

Figure 12.1 Types of mentoring programmes

The challenge of inter-company cross-mentoring programmes is to develop a cross-mentoring practice that responds to the same objectives as multi-site in-house cross-mentoring, with a stronger benchmark and network dimension. These cross-mentoring programmes, whether individual or collective, are often aimed at staying competitive, remaining attractive on the market and increasing employee loyalty and engagement. Maintaining the company's attractiveness as an employer brand, and learning from other businesses and organisations, help it to stay on track and renew itself.

In-house or inter-company cross-mentoring programmes particularly address the following dimension: the creation of new models of management and leadership suitable for our multicultural, interconnected world. Table 12.1 shows the range of mentoring practices. We are engaged in constant development, a dynamic of change and permanent adaptability as the norm. It is not an easy place in which to live and work, since it affects our reference points and habits, creating stress in our daily work.

There is a constant search for efficiency, looking for new practices, models of leadership and ways of addressing company management and its lifeblood: the employees! It is not easy to manage hierarchy and cooperative cultures at the same time. How can the historic, hierarchical order of companies, the need to improve performance and efficiency, be reconciled with employees' demands for greater flexibility and cooperation, more communications and well-being in the workplace?

In other words, how can we find the best way to work in order to succeed, perform and flourish? That is what mentoring programmes allow, in questioning and sharing responses and solutions that come from those on the ground. How do we work today? In what way? What direction should businesses take?

Table 12.1   Deployment of mentoring in organisations

	Within the company	Inter-entity multi-site	Inter-company
Collective cross-mentoring	X	X	X
Collective mentoring	X	X	(1)
Individual cross-mentoring	X	X	(1)

Note: (1) Deployment options according to the suitability of the programme.

What is the best form of governance? How do we respond to the needs of the market, to customers? How can we best use the variety of talents and skills available to create innovation? How do we train managers and decision-makers well?

brilliant impact

Mentoring programmes are a way of working directly on the ecology of performance: a set of levers to be activated and operate so that the company works and can perform well (Figure 12.2).

Figure 12.2 Ecology of performance

For your company to operate, it has to manage its talented people well: increase their skills, and capitalise on the experience and the expertise of its employees. Training is a good way of keeping employees up to date. No company today can guarantee jobs for its employees in the long term. There are too many uncertainties in the marketplace and the way the global economy operates. But your company is responsible for helping you improve your employability for job-seeking. All forms of individual and collective support must be used to achieve this. Training and managing talented people are essential if a company is to remain competitive. Developing a vision and putting it into effect form part of the ecology of performance. Without a vision, there is no helm to steer your company, no proper risk management and focused decision-making, no shared meaning or strategy worthy of the name or a really motivating challenge! Mentoring lets you work on all performance levers. Mentors and mentees, whether you meet in individual or collective mentoring programmes, you exchange your views on and experiences of the way this performance ecology operates. Mentors and mentees, the mentoring programmes that you are offered are special opportunities for you to act in a concrete way on all the parameters of your performance. Mentoring is the only tool that lets you work on all the factors that comprise performance.

Nowadays, mentoring has been boosted by the growth in social networks and the everyday use of NICT – New Information and Communications Technology – in our professional and personal environments. In this context, mentoring is part of a continuing process to break down as many barriers as possible, so it can be deployed across all these platforms (Figure 12.3).

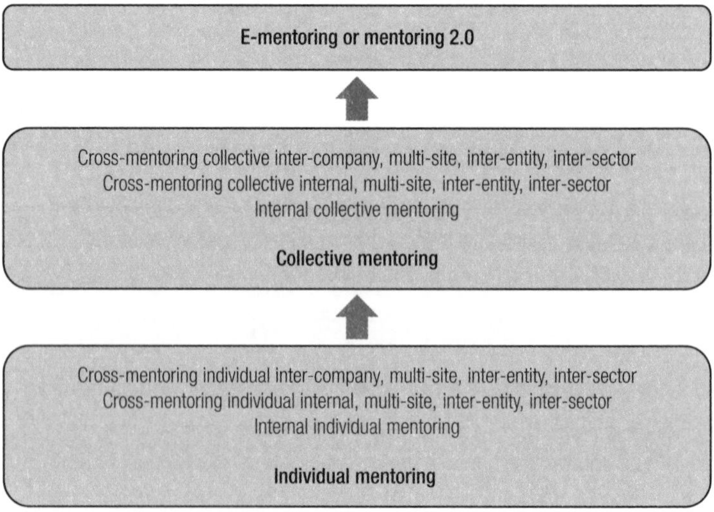

E-mentoring or mentoring 2.0

Cross-mentoring collective inter-company, multi-site, inter-entity, inter-sector
Cross-mentoring collective internal, multi-site, inter-entity, inter-sector
Internal collective mentoring

Collective mentoring

Cross-mentoring individual inter-company, multi-site, inter-entity, inter-sector
Cross-mentoring individual internal, multi-site, inter-entity, inter-sector
Internal individual mentoring

Individual mentoring

Figure 12.3 Development of mentoring

E-mentoring

Every new mentoring programme adds a further dimension of complexity that it incorporates by formalising a specific methodology to support participants and those initiating the mentoring.

E-mentoring is the most advanced form of mentoring in technical terms. E-mentoring is carried out on digital discussion platforms where mentors and mentees interact. These platforms can be extra to the physical meetings of mentor and mentees, or they can stand alone, overcoming the constraints of physical distance.

E-mentoring is found on online sharing forums, the intranets of businesses, business schools, universities, non-governmental organisations and associations for expatriates. It is also found in projects to support entrepreneurs who offer a cross-mentoring programme and want to increase the profile of their activities. Mentoring 2.0 can help recruit participants, spread information, share resources and enliven and animate multiple mentoring communities.

There is an important series of questions to ask. Once participants have completed mentoring programmes, what do we do with these communities of mentors and mentees working in businesses and organisations to improve performance and encourage a culture of cooperation? What do we do with these communities that develop a collaborative spirit in the professional support of their colleagues? The mentoring culture relies on strong values of sharing and transfer of all the knowledge that forms your professional identity. Mentoring offers a whole range of unique learning processes and enriches both mentors and mentees.

The digital community platform is one response which has the benefit of giving a second life to mentoring programmes, prolonging and capitalising on all the benefits of the programme for mentors and mentees once they have been trained and experienced. It is a way of re-resourcing all the participants by giving a digital visibility to those who have already given their time and commitment to these programmes. For organisations, it is also a way of building quality over the long term.

In cross-mentoring programmes, use of a digital platform helps in exchanges and resolves the problem of availability and diary management of the participants. It gives greater freedom by significantly reducing physical and geographical limitations. Virtualisation expands transmission possibilities and extends collaboration in the exchanges between mentors and mentees. It also increases the number of potential participants. For instance, a mentor hotline can be set up. Mentors can mentor several mentees and mentees have the chance to talk to several mentors, depending on their professional needs and environments. Mentor circles can be formed, along with mentee communities.

In general, e-mentoring does not replace mentoring programmes where mentors and mentees actually meet in person. E-mentoring is an extra tool, another way of overcoming diary and geographical restrictions and multiplying both resources and participants. It gives greater scope to programmes, so they can be applied at on a wider scale.

E-mentoring is part of the current trend driven by NICT, which affects how we work: the creation of new types of community. It involves the search for new forms of collaboration that extend the available resources and eliminate physical and geographical constraints to create a kind of universal time. Digital mentoring communities make people available to share knowledge, transmit, learn and give meaning to their work and activities. These communities collect their resources in professional cooperation networks that are aimed at both progress and well-being in learning.

E-learning, MOOC, e-research, e-science, the cyber-infrastructure, a hackathon are other examples of digital communities that share resources, expand knowledge and offer opportunities for cross-collaboration.

brilliant recap

In this chapter, these are the main things you should remember and understand about mentoring programmes:

1 Mentoring programmes adapt to the needs and challenges of your business.

2 The broad range of mentoring programmes enables integration of complexity and the many challenges of your business. Whether you are incorporating new subsidiaries in your company or you are seeking cohesion at a regional or a global level for your practices and core values, mentoring will help you to find solutions and put proper action plans in place.

3 Mentoring programmes increase individual and collective performance.

4 Mentoring programmes work directly on the ecology of performance.

5 Mentoring, cross-mentoring and e-mentoring programmes will develop you and your company in an efficient and innovative way. All these frameworks of mentoring offer high quality resources, process and methodology to help you face your needs and challenges.

Conclusion

Mentoring is an opportunity for our companies, organisations, institutions and for society on a broader scale. Why? Because it allows us to express and practise what we do best and forms the basis of all collective and individual effective empowerment: creating links, transmitting, engaging, recognising and being recognised. Individual and collective mentoring programmes give our companies positive impetus to develop systems of collaborative exchange, to improve performance and professional practices with the individual at the centre, while enabling the workers to do what they are paid for: working.

For your businesses and organisations, there is a dual benefit: your employees progress, communicate and share in an open environment, free of hierarchical stress. With mentoring help, they make their businesses, administrations and institutions more human as they progress.

Mentoring is a caring, ethical way of recognising the value of individuals as a quality resource for developing performance. Mentoring is enriching and rewarding for all participants, whether mentors or mentees. Mentoring helps to reinforce the strengths of your professional identity and boosts your career. Being a mentor will enrich you, just as being a mentee will also enrich you. The balanced, equal mentoring relationship contributes positively to the company, unlike solitary thinking and fixed hierarchies.

Today, we are immersed in an ever-deeper pool of digitisation of information and communication. The flourishing of social networks, internal and external professional networks and the internet, influence the way we communicate and have access to knowledge. New ways of working then emerge, new ways of seeing career paths, being evaluated, developing professionally, being visible, communicating, designing a strategy or exploring new markets, all with the common denominator: the drive for continual adaptation.

Developing individual and collective mentoring programmes meets the need to find solutions for this new order, starting from the ground up, from the experience and knowledge of people themselves. It is necessary to maintain and develop economic growth in your company, while optimising management of individual and collective performance. What is valuable is the approach offered by all mentoring programmes: a logic of qualitative, caring empowerment, aligned on professional objectives which participants feel as something other than training or an nth evaluation of their performance.

Nor is mentoring a Trojan horse, forcing individuals to progress and perform without their knowing it. It is a much broader economic and social project: combining ethics and well-being realistically in a model of growth, while enhancing as much as possible processes of cooperation and sharing. Mentors and mentees adapt, use and mobilise the best of their human qualities to grow professionally and give their organisations a new inspiration. This explains the success of these programmes in our companies, and we can only congratulate ourselves on their steady spread through organisations and institutions. It could be said that mentoring contributes to the creation of professional environments based on greater diversity and equality.

We have chosen to introduce you in a practical way to the various components of mentoring programmes, with the aim also of clarifying our complex systems and making them simpler and more comprehensible, easier to manage and ultimately reliable.

What did you think of this book?

We're really keen to hear from you about this book, so that we can make our publishing even better.

Please log on to the following website and leave us your feedback.

It will only take a few minutes and your thoughts are invaluable to us.

www.pearsoned.co.uk/bookfeedback

Bibliography

Arendt, Hannah (1999) *The Human Condition*, 2nd revised edition, Chicago: University of Chicago Press.

Dupuy, François (2011) *Lost in Management*, Paris: Seuil.

Ensher, Ellen and Murphy, Susan (2005) *Power Mentoring: How Successful Mentors and Proteges Get the Most Out of Their Relationships*, San Francisco: Jossey-Bass.

Honneth, Axel (1995) *The Struggle for Recognition: The Moral Grammar of Social Conflicts*, Cambridge: Polity Press.

Johnson, Harold E. (1997) *Mentoring for Exceptional Performance*, Glendale, California: Griffin Publishing Group.

Marzano, Michela (2010) *Extension du domaine de la manipulation: De l'entreprise à la vie privée*, Paris: Fayard/Pluriel.

Peter, Laurence J. and Hull, Raymond (2011) *The Peter Principle*, London: Harper Business, Reprint edition.

Senge, Peter (2006) *The Fifth Discipline: The Art and Practice of the Learning Organization*, 2nd revised edition, New York: Random House Business.

Sloterdijk, Peter (1989) *Eurotaoismus. Zur Kritik der politischen Kinetik*, Frankfurt am Main: Suhrkamp.

Thomas, Kenneth W. and Velthouse, Betty A. (1990) 'Cognitive elements of empowerment: an "interpretive" model of intrinsic task motivation', *The Academy of Management Review*, 15(4): 666–81.

Tsunetomo, Yamamoto (1979) *Hagakure: The Book of the Samurai,* trans. William Scott Wilson, Kondansha International Ltd.

Index

Do you want your people to be the very best at what they do?

Talk to us about how we can help.

As the world's leading learning company, we know a lot about what your people need in order to be better at what they do.

Whatever subject or skills you've got in mind (from presenting or persuasion to coaching or communication skills), and at whatever level (from new-starters through to top executives) we can help you deliver tried-and-tested, essential learning straight to your workforce – whatever they need, whenever they need it and wherever they are.

Talk to us today about how we can:

- Complement and support your existing learning and development programmes
- Enhance and augment your people's learning experience
- Match your needs to the best of our content
- Customise, brand and change it to make a better fit
- Deliver cost-effective, great value learning content that's proven to work.

Contact us today:
corporate.enquiries@pearson.com